PRAISE: A WAY OF LIFE

Praise:

a way of life

Paul Hinnebusch, O. P.

Servant Books
Ann Arbor, Michigan

Quotations from St. John of the Cross are taken from the *Collected Works of St. John of the Cross,* translated by Kieran Kavanaugh and Otilio Rodriguez. Copyright © 1964 by Washington Province of Discalced Carmelites, Inc. Paperback edition published by ICS Publications, Washington, D.C., U.S.A.

ISBN 0-89283-032-8

Printed in the United States of America

To my brothers and sisters of the Christian Community of God's Delight, Dallas, Texas, whose daily prayers for God's blessing upon the writing of this book were generously answered.

ACKNOWLEDGEMENT

My sincere gratitude to all my brothers and sisters in the Lord who have lovingly spent time and effort and prayer in responding to my request for their witness concerning praise in their lives, and to Miss Viola R. Bezner for beautifully typing the manuscript.

REFERENCES

Except where otherwise indicated, we have used *The Holy Bible, Revised Standard Version*, copyright 1946 and 1952 by the Division of Christian Education of the National Council of the Churches of Christ in the U.S.A. Quotations from other versions are indicated by these symbols after the references:

  b—The latest French edition of *La Bible de Jérusalem* (Nouvelle edition entièrement revue et augmentée). (Paris: du Cerf, 1973)

  d—Douay-Rheims

  j—*The Jerusalem Bible*, copyright 1966 by Doubleday and Company, Inc.

  k—The King James Version

  n—*The New American Bible*, copyright 1970 by the Confraternity of Christian Doctrine, Washington, D.C.

  w—Artur Weiser, *The Psalms* (Philadelphia:Westminister, 1962).

  r—Revised Standard Version

DS—When used after a quotation indicates *Dictionnaire de Spiritualite* (Paris: Beauchesne), 1935-1975.

PL—Migne: Patres Latini

CONTENTS

To Love and to Praise

When we enjoy something, we spontaneously praise it: "What a glorious sunset!" "What a delicious dinner!" Just as spontaneously, we invite others to join us in this praise: "Isn't she lovely?" "Wasn't that a beautiful song?" And we want to hear a heartfelt "Yes" to this. Our own enjoyment of what we love is not complete till others enjoy and praise it with us.

More ardent praise breaks forth into song. "Singing comes from joy," says Augustine. "But if we observe more carefully, it comes from love. You want to sing about what you love!"[1] Singing, a natural expression of love and praise, has an irreplaceable role in Christian worship, in which we love the Lord our God with all our heart and soul and mind and strength. God created us that we might have joy in loving him, and this joy, like all joy, overflows as praise.

When, therefore, God requires that we praise him, he is really inviting us to love and enjoy him. For no love and joy is complete till it is expressed in praise. In describing us as "the people whom I formed for myself that they might announce my praise" (Isa. 43:21 *n*),

1

God is not an egotistical, self-centered God demanding compliments and adulation. He is a humble, loving, outgoing God who keeps nothing to himself, but reveals all his beauty and perfection to us for our loving enjoyment. He shares himself totally that we might have joy in his presence, joy in loving communion with him.

Praise is our joyous response to God's glorious self-giving. That is why St. Paul says that God does everything "for the praise of his glorious grace" (Eph. 1:6). It is impossible to taste the magnificent goodness of God without responding in joyous praise.

To say then that God wants our praise is to say that he wants us to have the glorious joy of loving him and living in intimate communion with him. "He chose us in Christ that we should be holy and blameless in his presence in love . . . to the praise of his glorious grace which he freely bestowed on us in the Beloved" (Eph. 1:4-6).

We are a people of praise because we are a people who love and enjoy our God. "You are a chosen race, a royal priesthood, a consecrated nation, a people set apart *to sing the praises of God* who called you out of the darkness into his wonderful light" (1 Pet. 2:9 *j*). Our coming into full possession of our inheritance as God's children results in "the praise of his glory" (Eph. 1:14). "We have been destined and appointed to live for the praise of his glory" (Eph.1:12).

Because God formed us as a people to announce his praise, we are not fully Christian if we are not expressing our joy in praise. Praise is the Christian way of life because love and joy are the Christian way of life. Love grows and deepens only if it is expressed. Perhaps we have not grown in love and joy because we have failed to express our love and joy in praise. Love and praise call for each other. Augustine says, "To love and to praise: to praise in love, and to love in praise. 'Happy they who dwell in your house! Continually they praise you!' (Ps. 84:5)."[2]

Praise As A Way Of Life

This book could have been subtitled "A Spirituality of Praise." By "a spirituality" I mean a way of life, a way of living the life in the Spirit. The spirituality of praise says: "Enjoy God to the full! Express your love for him in hearty praise!" Praise is simply enjoying our God.

This praise, however, is an ingredient which penetrates the totality of fervent Christian life, in the way that leaven penetrates the whole dough. Praise in word and song is completed only in a life which is praise.

Praise as a way of life is well described by Augustine in these words:

> "Sing to the Lord a new song." Sing with your voice, your mouth, your hearts, sing with befitting behavior. "May his praise ring out in the gathering of the saints." The singer himself is the praise that must be sung. Do you want to praise God? You are the praise that must be said. You are his praise if you live righteously.[3]

Praise spirituality is community spirituality. "Singing manifests and fosters love among brothers," says Pope Paul VI. "The community is formed in singing, assisting the blending of hearts with that of voices, eliminating

3

the differences of age, origin, and social background, uniting everyone in a single aspiration of praise to God, Creator of the universe and Father of all" (September, 1972).[4]

How This Book Came To Be

This book had its origins in a community of praise in Dallas, a community which was "formed in singing," *The Christian Community of God's Delight.* God delights in those who praise him, because he rejoices in the joy of those who love him. Mr. Bobbie J. Cavnar, the leader of this community, is well known for "the festal shout" (Ps.89:16). Wherever he speaks, he urges people to acclaim the Lord with loud praise, pointing to the fruitful experience of his own community. In a remarkable way, vocal praise has opened the hearts of these people to the action of the Holy Spirit, and has produced indisputable fruits of Christian holiness in the community.

Mr. Cavnar first asked me to write this book. Shortly afterwards, two different publishers wrote to me, urging me to write it, because both of them had heard Mr. Cavnar speak so eloquently about praise. One of these, Mr. Bert Ghezzi of Word of Life, recommended that I write not only about loud praise, but also about the many other forms in which praise of God is expressed. He suggested that I present all of this in the framework of the history of praise.

I replied, saying that I had no inclination to do the research necessary for a history of praise. But after mailing my letter to him, I opened a package which had

4

arrived that day from France. It was the latest volume of *Dictionnaire de Spiritualité*. I opened it to an article entitled, "Jubilation."[5]

Jubilation is an especially exuberant joy in praising God. It has been so important in Jewish and Christian spirituality that it merited a special article in the encyclopedia. The article provided me with a sketchy outline of the history of praise by tracing the evolution of the experience of jubilation as described in the Bible and in the great writers of Christian spirituality. The article thus furnished me with multiple clues which lured me into writing this book.

As I studied the article, I realized that ever so much of the history of praise is being renewed and repeated among my charismatic friends. Therefore I asked these friends to tell me what praise means in their lives, what fruits it produces, what forms it takes. For I felt that anything I would write about the history of praise would be relevant today only if I could show how it is still happening in the lives of people today. Therefore the book is interspersed with the witness of these friends concerning the role of praise in their lives.

This book is not a complete history of praise. I merely give examples here and there from history to show that the forms of contemporary praise are not without precedent. What is happening now has happened before. Christians of the present have no monopoly on the workings of the Holy Spirit. And our own experience of praise can be greatly enriched by what we learn from those who went before us.

Thus, the book presents not only words of witness from the people of praise today, but hopes also to encourage these people to grow in more wonderful ways of praising by presenting some of the witness of great men and women of praise in the past: the psalmists; the evangelists—especially St. Luke; the Fathers of the Church—especially St. Augustine; and more modern writers such as Teresa of Avila and John of the Cross.

My own reflections on this experience of the present and of the past might be called a theology of praise, or better, a spirituality of praise, a way of Christian living.

Not one of my friends whose witness appears in this book saw in advance even one word of what I have written about praise. Therefore, their witness is independent of mine, completely uninfluenced by my research and reflections. Most of this witness is presented in the latter half of the book.

I have used only the witness of people whom I know personally and for whose veracity I can vouch. True Christian witness is always inspired by love. Its whole purpose is to bring others to the Lord. All these witnesses whom I quote spoke prompted by love, and love accepts the truth of what they say. Each of these witnesses can make the sentiments of Augustine his own:

> Those will believe this witness whose ears are open in love, because 'love believes all things' that are spoken in love. The love by which my hearers are good tells them that in my witness I do not lie about myself, and this love in them believes me.[6]

Sincere praise of God is the most effective antidote for boasting about self. All the witnesses whose word we present spoke only in praise of God, none of them were boasting about themselves. Witness to the wonders that God is doing in one's life is itself a way of praising God.

If Mr. Cavnar's love of "the festal shout" sparked the writing of this book, the article on jubilation in *Diction-*

naire de Spiritualité fanned the spark into flame. The English word "jubilation" derives from the Latin "jubilatio," which translates a Hebrew word in the Bible which meant "the festal shout." Jubilation, the festal shout, is a key theme in this book, with other themes woven into a symphony around it. Beginning with the festal shout, the book ends by developing Augustine's theme, "*You* are the praise that must be sung. *You* are praise of God if you live righteously."

PART ONE

The Festal Shout

CHAPTER ONE

Jubilation:
"The Festal Shout"

There is no doubt that the Hebrew people were often quite loud in their praise of God. This is clear from two Hebrew words which occur frequently in the psalms, *ruwa* and *teruwah*.

Figuratively, *ruwa* means "to split the ears with sound; that is *to shout* (for alarm or joy); to make a joyful noise." "Make a joyful noise to God, all the earth" (Ps.66:1). "Shout to God with loud songs of joy" (Ps. 47:2).

From this verb is derived the noun *teruwah*, which means "clamor, that is, acclamation of joy, or a battle cry." "Blessed are the people who know the festal shout (*teruwah*)" (Ps.89:15).

When the Hebrew psalms were translated into Latin, these two words were rendered as *jubilare* and *jubilatio*, from which our word "jubilation" is derived.

There is an evolution in the meaning of the original Hebrew words in the Old Testament, and an evolution in the meaning of the Latin equivalents in the writings of

11

the Fathers of the Church and later Christian writers. This evolution in the meaning of the words corresponds to an evolution in the Hebrew and Christian experience of God. Jubilation in its various forms and degrees is a manifestation of this deepening experience of God.

In the light of the history of this evolution, we shall reflect upon the current experience of loud praise in contemporary charismatic communities. But more important than that, we shall try to show the value of praise in every Christian life.

Jubilation is perhaps the truest and purest of all forms of praise of God, because it is centered directly on the very presence of God. It is a joyous acclamation of the Lord, welcoming him into our midst. It results from a deep experience of his presence. It is a tasting of God; it is joy that he is what he is; it is delight in God precisely because he is God. It is an interior spiritual joy which is usually irrepressible, yet inexpressible in words. Therefore it breaks forth exteriorly in wordless cries and chants, and sometimes in dance.

The speaking in tongues and singing in the Spirit which are so characteristic of contemporary charismatic communities are forms of jubilation.

The Battle Cry

Even in its primitive biblical forms, jubilation was centered on the presence of God. Originally the word *teruwah* signified the war cry that preluded attack (Josh.6:5, Exod.32:17). This war cry was in reality a religious rite, for it was an acclamation of Yahweh, the God of Israel, present with his people to lead them in battle, forwarding his purposes on their behalf. Thus, the battle cry was an act of faith in God. It saluted Yahweh as King and leader in war: "Yahweh his God is with him (the people of Israel); in him (the people) sounds the royal acclaim (*teruwah*)" (Num.23:21*j*).

The battle cry (*teruwah*) was called forth by a command, by the sound of a trumpet: "When they make a long blast with the ram's horn, as soon as you hear the sound of the trumpet, then all the people shall *shout with a great shout (teruwah)* and the wall of the city will fall down flat" (Josh.6:5). "When the ark of the covenant of the Lord came into the camp, all Israel gave *a mighty shout,* so that the earth resounded" (1 Sam.4:5). God had seen fit often to manifest his presence powerfully wherever the ark of the covenant was venerated by his people, and so the *teruwah,* as a cry greeting the ark, was an acclamation of God himself present with his people.

True, the people of Israel may sometimes have performed the religious rite of the *teruwah* as if it were a magical formula. On one occasion when the armies of Israel were being defeated by the Philistines, the Israelites hastened to bring the ark of the covenant to the battle field, expecting this to bring them certain victory. They greeted it with the mighty shout (1 Sam.4). But God, by allowing the ark to be captured by the enemy, cured his people of expecting magical results. The people had to learn that only genuine faith in the Lord, faithfulness to his covenant, and obedience to his moral will would guarantee that the Lord would remain with them to win their battles.

Therefore after the captured ark had been miraculously returned (1 Sam.6), the prophet Samuel gathered the people together to renew their faith in Yahweh and

13

to restore them in faithfulness to his will. "Samuel said to all the house of Israel, 'If you are returning to the Lord with all your heart, then put away the foreign gods and the ashtaroth from among you, and direct your heart to the Lord, and serve him only, and he will deliver you out of the hand of the Philistines'" (1 Sam. 7:3).

Loud priase does not work like magic. To win the presence of God, it must be sincere, from the heart, and an expression of genuine faith and trust. It must be accompanied by a sincere will for conversion of heart and for purity of morals. Praise without obedience is hollow. "When I appealed to the Lord in words, praise was under my tongue. Were I to cherish wickedness in my heart, the Lord would not hear; but God has heard; he has hearkened to the sound of my prayer. Blessed be God who refused me not my prayer or his kindness" (Ps.66:17-20n).

The Festal Acclamation

The ritual battle hurrah later took on a liturgical character. The evolution of the *teruwah* from its use in a ritual of war to usage in liturgical worship is evident in Psalm 33. "Shout for joy to Yahweh ... Play to him on the ten-string harp ... Play with all your skill *as you hail him with the war cry (teruwah)*" (Ps.33:1-3j). Because of the evolution in the meaning of *teruwah*, the last phrase is more accurately rendered *"as you acclaim him in worship."* The loud battle shout has become a liturgical acclamation: "Blessed are the people who know the festal shout *(teruwah)*" (Ps.89:15). This is also translated, "Happy the people who learn to *acclaim* you" (Ps.89:15j).

It is still a shout, an acclamation expressed with deep feeling. The psalmist is not simply using poetic language when he says, "Make a joyful noise to God" (Ps.66:1). Literal loud praise was part of the Israelite religous experience. The festal shout was officially prescribed for certain liturgical occasions. Trumpets called forth loud acclamations from the people; for example, on the autumn festival which eventually became the Jewish New Year's Day: "On the first day of the seventh month you shall have a holy convocation . . . It is a day for you to blow the trumpets" (Num.29:1). This feast of trumpets was a day of acclamation of God present with his people: "Sing aloud to God our strength, shout for joy to the God of Jacob . . . Blow the trumpet at the new moon, at the full moon, on our feast day" (Ps.81:1-3).

The *teruwah* was used also at sacrifices of thanksgiving (Ps.27:6; 65:13) and at procession liturgies: "O come let us sing to the Lord, let us make *a joyful noise (teruwah)* to the Rock of our salvation. *Let us come into his presence* with thanksgiving, let us make a joyful noise to him with songs of praise. For the Lord is a great God, and a King above all gods" (Ps.95:1-3).

Joy in God's Presence

Jubilation, the festal shout, is always an acclamation of the Lord himself, and expresses joy in his presence. It celebrates what the Lord is in himself, even more than his deeds on behalf of men. It results from some kind of experience of the Lord, a tasting of his goodness.

That the *teruwah*, or jubilation, is an acclamation of the very presence of God is manifest in the poetic parallelism of these verses:

> Blessed are the people who know the festal shout, who walk, O Lord, in the light of thy countenance; they exult in they Name all the day, they are exalted in thy righteousness. (Ps.89:15-16)

The four lines are more or less synonyms, expressing four aspects of one same reality. "They walk, O Lord, in the light of thy countenance"; that is, God's people live in his presence, they enjoy his loving favor towards them. "They exult in thy name": that is, they rejoice in his personal presence (in the Bible, "the Name" signifies a presence of God; God's Name, for example, is said to dwell in the sanctuary (2 Kings 21:27), for it is there that he manifests his presence in a special way). "They are exalted in thy righteousness"; that is, His people are lifted up in joy, because of his righteousness. As an attribute of his covenant faithfulness, God's righteousness is a quality of his very person; and to rejoice in his righteousness is to rejoice in the Lord himself.

The festal shout, then, is a response to the experienced presence of the Lord; it is an acclamation of the Lord who is with his people. The people are filled with jubilation because they experience communion with the divine Majesty.

Or, at least, the festal shout in the worshipping assembly is a preparation opening the people to this presence of God. Certainly the psalms were composed by persons who had experienced this presence, and are a witness and call to others to come into it:

16

Make a joyful noise *(teruwah)* to the Lord, all the lands! Serve the Lord with gladness! Come into his presence with singing! ... For the Lord is good, his steadfast love endures forever, and his faithfulness to all generations." (Ps.100)

This psalm expresses all the elements of which we have been speaking, and sums up beautifully the nature of Jewish and Christian praise.

Lord And Judge Of The Nations

It is quite plausible that it was during the liturgy of praise in the temple that Isaiah was granted his vision of Yahweh as King of the nations, filling all the earth with his glory (Isa.6:1-7). The liturgy was presided over by Yahweh's presence, symbolized by the ark of the covenant in the Holy of Holies. But Isaiah's vision contained a new divine revelation. Isaiah sees Yahweh not simply as enthroned in Israel over the ark, but as Lord and King of all the earth: "Holy, holy, holy is the Lord of hosts: the whole earth is full of his glory!" (Isa.6:3).

The Lord is present in all the earth, and psalm after psalm calls upon all the earth to acclaim him with the festal shout: "O sing to the Lord a new song, for he has done marvelous things! All the ends of the earth have seen the victory of our God. Make *a joyful noise* to the Lord, all the earth" (Ps.98). Praise of God must become universal; God is judge of the nations: "Clap your hands, all you peoples! Shout *(ruwa)* to God with loud songs of joy! For the Lord, the Most High, is terrible, a great king over all the earth ... God has gone up with a shout

17

(*teruwah*), the Lord with the sound of a trumpet. Sing praises to God, sing praises! Sing praises to our King, sing praises!" (Ps.47:1-6).

The Judge of the Nations is acclaimed with joy, because he is a redeeming God who delivers his people. The old Israelite concept of "the Day of the Lord" as a divine intervention of God rescuing his people from their military foes evolved, in the days of the prophets, into the notion of God intervening to bring his own people to judgment. But in either case, it is the same God whose presence is experienced. The festal shout of the seraphim in Isaiah's vision, "Holy, holy, holy," is an expression of most profound awe and holy fear in the presence of "the Holy One of Israel," for God is exercising judgment upon his people (e.g., Isa.5:15-16). The acclamation, "Holy, holy, holy is the Lord God of hosts" (Isa.6:3), results from an intimate experience of the deepest nature of God's holiness, and makes the prophet realize his own and his people's need of purification before they can live in his presence (Isa.6:5).

Thus, though the experience of the Lord often brings a festal joy, when his presence is experienced at another depth, it results in a holy fear and a cry for a deeper purification of one's heart and lips (Isa.6:5-7). Isaiah witnesses the festal shout of the heavenly seraphim, but cannot yet join in with it, till he is purified by the burning coal from the altar of sacrifice. Acceptable praise springs from purified hearts and lips.

This, too, is the experience of charismatic prayer communities. Calls for growth in holiness repeatedly come to them from the Lord. "Praise was on the tip of my tongue. Were I to cherish wickedness in my heart, the Lord would not hear" (Ps.66:17-18n).

In the Christian Eucharistic celebration, the "holy,

holy, holy" of Isaiah is now used as an acclamation of
the Holy Trinity. By sharing in the sacrifice of the Lord
Jesus, Christians can live in the presence of the thrice
holy One, their hearts purified by the burning coal of
love, which is the Holy Spirit poured out into their
hearts from the altar of the Lord Jesus.

The Christian Invitatory

Because the *teruwah* was originally a loud war cry,
someone may be inclined to reject the festal shout as
being too primitive for contemporary Americans. Loud
praise is often disdained as unrefined, excessively emotional, lacking in good taste, offending the sensibilities of
many prayerful people, and flying in the face of the
many centuries of more recent and more developed
spiritual experience, in which God has been deeply
experienced in silence and in solitude.

But is loud praise primitive? The history of jubilation
which we shall trace through the Christian centuries
shows that jubilation has survived among Christians even
into modern times, and in those very monasteries where
silent contemplative prayer was cultivated in solitude. We
shall note, for example, the exuberance of John of the
Cross when the Lord touched him with his marvelous
presence. And St. Teresa of Avila not only expects that
there will be exuberant praise of God in monasteries, she
says that monasteries are the place where one who
praises God with exuberance is most likely to be understood and accepted. Here are her words concerning a
God-given "jubilation, a strange kind of prayer ... an
entirely supernatural thing which we cannot acquire by
our own efforts":

19

The joy of the soul in this jubilation is so exceedingly great that it would like, not to rejoice in God in solitude, but to tell its joy to all, so that they may help it praise our Lord, to which end it directs its whole activity.... Impelled as it is by this great joy, the soul cannot be expected to keep silence and dissemble....

How fortunate to be in a convent, where people won't speak against you if you praise God in this way, but will encourage you to praise him the more....

Sometimes it makes me specially glad when we are together and I see these sisters of mine so full of inward joy that each vies with the rest in praising our Lord.... I should like you to praise him often, sisters, for when one of you begins to do so, she arouses the rest. How can your tongues be better employed when you are together than in the praises of God, which we have so many reasons for rendering him?

The real truth is that this joy makes the soul so forgetful of itself, and of everything, that it is conscious of nothing, and able to speak of nothing, save of that which proceeds from its joy, namely, the praises of God. Let us join with this soul, my daughters all. Why should we want to be more sensible than she? What can give us greater pleasure than to do as she does? And may all the creatures join with us forever and ever. Amen, amen, amen![7]

Jubilation in some form is to be expected especially in the silent monastic life, for daily the monks and nuns invite one another into the presence of the Lord, as they sing together the Invitatory, the great song of acclamation, which for many centuries has been the official opening ceremony in the Church's daily liturgy of praise: "Come, ring out our joy to the Lord, let us acclaim (*teruwah*) the Rock of our salvation. Let us greet him with thanksgiving, let us joyfully sing psalms to him" (Ps.95:1n). It is only to be expected that joy and jubilation will be normal where this ceremony, built around Psalm 95, is carried out in alert seriousness.

I have noted, too, how consistently the prayer assemblies of the Christian Community of God's Delight in Dallas begin with an invitatory, words of invitation to enjoy the Lord's presence: "We gather here each Sunday evening to have a good time singing before our God." Praise of God is something which is deeply enjoyed by these people. Christianity is a religion of joy. Burdens and worries fade away because they are entrusted to the Lord in loving faith.

Though among the Jews the *teruwah* of jubilation was a liturgical ceremony, it expressed a very exalted interior attitude: the adoration of God, Lord and King present with his people, and thanksgiving to him as Savior of his people. This liturgy of praise was carried out in full expectation of meeting this Lord in faith, and of tasting the sweetness of his presence: "I will bless the Lord at all times, his praises shall continually be in my mouth ... O taste and see that the Lord is good!" (Ps. 34:1,8). Such, too, is the faith and expectation of contemporary charismatics as they invite one another to praise the Lord.

Praise Of God And Openness To His Word

Liturgical music and singing has a power to arouse in

man the spirit of true worship of God, and to open him to the Word and Spirit of God. In the midst of the liturgical singing in the Jewish temple worship, the presence of God was frequently manifested in various graces of deep communion with him (cf., 2 Chron.5: 13-14). Often, explicit oracles would be received from the Lord in consequence of the festal acclamations of his presence. Many psalms contain evidence of this response by God to hymns of praise.

For example, after the call for loud praise of God in Psalm 81:1-6, the psalmist abruptly says, "An unfamiliar speech I hear" (Ps.81:6n). No doubt he has heard a word from God. He goes on to proclaim a message in which God speaks in the first person to his people, and calls for a more faithful response to his word.

Psalm 95 likewise, after exhorting the people to acclaim the presence of the Lord, to hail him who is in their midst, appeals to them to listen to his voice today and not to harden their hearts (Ps. 95:7).

A number of the psalms contain words or oracles received from God in his sanctuary. Usually these are received in the setting of praise and thanksgiving, and often in response to a cry of distress which is accompanied by praise (Ps.2:6, 12:5, 60:6, 75:2, 82:2). One psalmist, for example, tortured by the problem of unrequited evil, receives divine enlightenment concerning his problem when he comes into the divine presence in the sanctuary: "But when I thought how to understand this, it seemed to me a wearisome task, until I went into the sanctuary of God; then I perceived their end" (Ps.73: 16-17).

Sometimes in a psalm of lamentation, there is a hiatus, an empty place between the cry of distress and the song of thanksgiving. At this point, God has spoken in the heart. Psalm 22, for example, is a long lamentation (1-21), followed by a song of praise (22-31). In the Hebrew text, the lamentation ends abruptly with the words, "You have heard me!" (Ps.22:21), and praise follows immediately.

All of this seems evidence enough that in the Jewish liturgy of praise God often spoke explicitly to his people, either in the depths of their hearts, or in vocal oracles like the words of prophecy which he gives in the midst of praise in contemporary charismatic prayer communities.

CHAPTER TWO

The Christian Festal Shout

The transition of the *teruwah* from a war cry to a liturgical acclamation, we said, reflects a deepening of Israel's experience of God. Early faith in Yahweh had often been expressed in the imagery of a warrior king leading his people into battle. The more experienced faith of later generations thought of him as the spiritual king, the one and only King of all the nations. Thus, the word *teruwah*, "joyful noise," received a new content when it was transformed from war cry into a liturgical acclamation of the presence of the Lord.

Another profound change in man's experience of this one same God took place when the Son of God became man and dwelt among us, and remained among us after his resurrection as "Son of God in power, Jesus Christ our Lord" (Rom.1:4). The God of Israel has been experienced in a new way in the risen Lord, and in the power of his resurrection working in his people. Therefore the word *teruwah*, or rather its Latin equivalent in the psalms, *jubilatio*, receives a richer content than before when it is used to express Christian joy in the Lord's resurrection.

This is clear from the writings of the Fathers of the Church. They speak of jubilation as joy in the redemption brought to us by the risen Lord. Origen (died 254), for example, commenting on the words of Psalm 47— "God has gone up with a shout (*teruwah*), the Lord with the sound of a trumpet"—says that the shout is a song of victory, celebrating our hope of resurrection in Christ.

In the Latin Vulgate, moreover, and in some Greek manuscripts used by the early Christians, Psalm 66— "Make a joyful noise (teruwah) to God, all the earth"—is given the title, "A Psalm of the Resurrection." Without changing a word, Christians fill the words and imagery of the psalms with a new meaning, which is a profound deepening of the original meaning.

As originally written, Psalm 66 is a hymn to God's power as King of the nations. His power is so tremendous that all his enemies cower before him: "Acclaim God, all the earth ... Say to God, What dread you inspire! Your achievements are the measure of your power. Your enemies cringe in your presence" (Ps.66: 1-3*j*). In the French original of the Jerusalem Bible, the words are still more impressive: "Your works are measured by your power (A la mesure de ta force tes oeuvres)" (Ps.66*b*); that is, your power produces works to the full strength of that power. The psalmist seems to be saying, "Your power is not limited to the land of Israel. You use your power to the maximum in showing yourself king of the nations."

But when Christians use these words of the psalm, they are speaking of an experience of God's power infinitely exceeding all that the psalmist could have dreamed of. The words seem to be echoed by St. Paul's words concerning the power of the resurrection working in our hearts. Paul prays for us, asking "that you may know . . . what is the immeasurable greatness of his power in us who believe. (Its measure is) the working of his great might which he accomplished in Christ when he raised him from the dead, and made him sit at his right hand far above all rule and authority and power and dominion, and above every name that is named . . . and he has put all things under his feet . . ." (Eph.1:19-22).

Thus, we can estimate the greatness of what God is doing in us by the power of the Spirit which he exerted in raising Jesus from the dead and establishing him as Lord, Son of God in power (Rom.1:4). This is the power which is working in us who believe (Eph.1:19), elevating us with Christ to life with God (Eph.2:5-6). "Jesus is Lord!" (1 Cor.12:3; Phil.2:11), is the festal cry of a Christian.

The psalm speaks of the *glorious* praise which all nations must give to God for his *glorious* work (Ps.66: 2-3). Paul seems to echo this verse also. All that God is doing for us in Christ (Eph.1:3-14) is for "the praise of his *glorious* grace" (Eph.1:6).

Any Christian who has experienced the power of the risen Lord in his life can now use these old psalms with this new meaning. The imagery of the Red Sea and the Jordan in Psalm 66, for example, now expresses the Christian's joy in the risen Jesus and in the new exodus, the redemption being accomplished in us by his power as Lord: "Come and see what God has done: he is terrible in his deeds among men. He turned the sea into dry land, men passed through the river on foot. There did we rejoice in him who rules by his might forever, whose eyes keep watch on the nations" (Ps.66:5-7). Acclamation of the risen Lord, a cry of welcome to him and openness to his power, prepares the way for the effective establishment of this rule in the hearts of all men.

Jubilation, the festal shout, is no longer literally a primitive battle cry. It is a joyous cry of victory in Christ. It is an acclamation of the risen Lord present in our midst and acting with power in our lives. It is not necessarily a cry with all the power of one's lungs, though at times it is very fitting that it should be that. It is essentially a spiritual joy which finds expression in a variety of ways, corresponding to the manner and level and circumstances of the experience. This will become clear from our consideration of further witness to jubilation in the New Testament and in the writings of ancient and medieval Christians.

The wonderful new revival of the festal shout among so many of our contemporary Christians, "Jesus is Lord," is a sign that the Lord is about to assert his power among the nations in a wonderful way. The charismatic festal shout *expects* him to manifest his presence, and to exert his power in an *unexpected* way which will truly be astonishing.

CHAPTER THREE

St. Luke and the Festal Shout

Early Christian writers, we said, spoke of jubilation as joy in the risen Lord and in his redeeming power working in our midst. The Gospel of St. Luke, especially, rings from end to end with this joy.

Though God gave Jesus the title "Lord" only in his resurrection because of his obedience unto death (Phil. 2:11), Luke gives him this title throughout his Gospel, even in the Bethlehem story (Luke 2:11). This is because Jesus' redemptive power was already at work when he went about forgiving sins, healing the sick, raising the dead, preaching the good news to the poor. Each time that Luke tells of a manifestation of the Lord's power, he tells also of the joyous praise of God which bursts forth from the people. He joyfully records all the expressions of recognition of the Lord and joy in response to the blessings he brings.

Thus, the paralytic, whose sins Jesus forgave, rose from his bed and picked it up, "and went home *glorifying God*. And amazement seized them all, and they *glorified God*" (5:25-26). The Samaritan leper, "when he saw that he was healed, turned back, *praising God with a loud voice*" (17:15). "And immediately (the blind man) received his sight and followed him, *glorifying God*; and all the people when they saw it *gave praise to God*" (18:43). When the disciples experienced that they had a share in the Lord's healing power, they "returned *with joy*, saying, 'Lord, even the demons are subject to us in your name!' " (10:17). When Jesus cured the woman who had been bent over for eighteen years, "all the people *rejoiced* at all the glorious things that were done by him" (13:17). "The whole multitude of the disciples began *to rejoice and to praise God with a loud voice* for all the mighty works that they had seen" (19:37). "And they returned to Jerusalem *with great joy* and were *continually* in the temple *blessing God*" (24:52-53).

Truly, Luke's is the Gospel of joyous praise. The "loud voice" with which the people praised God is a continuation of the festal shout of Old Israel. This is evident from Luke's account of Mary's visit to Elizabeth:

> When Elizabeth heard the greeting of Mary, the babe leaped in her womb; and Elizabeth was filled with the Holy Spirit, and she exclaimed with *a loud cry*, "Blessed are you among women, and blessed is the fruit of your womb! And why is this granted me, that the mother of my Lord should come to me? For behold, when *the voice* of your greeting came to my ears, the babe in my womb leaped *for joy*" (Luke 1:41-44).

In telling this story in this way, St. Luke is referring us back to an event in the Old Testament. When David brought the ark of the covenant to his capital city, the people acclaimed the Lord "with shouting (*teruwah*) and with the sound of the horn" (2 Sam.6:15). The same Greek word used in the Greek Old Testament for *teruwah*, the liturgical acclamation used in greeting the Lord and the ark, is the Greek word used by St. Luke to describe Elizabeth's loud cry in greeting Mary.

And the word used in the Greek Old Testament for the sound of the trumpet announcing the presence of the ark and calling for the festal shout is the Greek word used by Luke to describe the sound of Mary's voice in greeting Elizabeth. Mary's greeting is the trumpet cry: "The Lord is here!" And Elizabeth's loud cry of joy is the festal shout, the acclamation greeting the Lord present in Mary's womb. Mary is the true ark of the covenant, and Jesus is the fulfillment of the Law which was kept in the ark. He is also the real presence of God which was symbolized by the ark.

The whole symphony of praise resounding throughout Luke's Gospel and continuing on into his Acts of the Apostles is thus presented by Luke as the festal shout acclaiming and welcoming the Lord God, present among his people in the person of Jesus, his son. "They glorified God, saying ... 'God has visited his people' " (Luke 7:16). Luke would have us all join in this festal shout, expressing our joy in the same Holy Spirit who inspired Mary's and Elizabeth's joyous parise.

The Magnificat

Elizabeth's festal shout sparks in turn Mary's great hymn of praise, the Magnificat (Luke 1:46-55). And the great symphony of joy thus begun has never ceased throughout the ages. From the earliest days of the Church, God's people have continued to sing Mary's song. In the seventh century, for example, St. Bede the Venerable (born 673) alludes to this custom in a homily on the Magnificat:

> For some time now the holy Church has had the splendid and holy custom whereby all daily sing the canticle of Mary in the psalmody of evening praise. . . . The office of vespers was rightly chosen for this canticle so that our mind which is fatigued by the labors of the day and still absorbed by the most varied thoughts might, with the approach of our nightly rest, collect itself in its innermost self. . . .
>
> "God who is mighty has done great things for me, and holy is his name" (Luke 1:49). Mary ascribes nothing to her own merits, but attributes all her greatness to God, who, great and powerful by nature, customarily lifts up his faithful from humility to greatness, from frailty to strength. And she fittingly adds, "Holy is his name," thus urging all her hearers, and all those who would be reached by her words, to have recourse with confidence to God in the psalmody of evening praise.[8]

Thirteen hundred years after St. Bede pointed out that the Church daily continues to sing Mary's own song of praise, Pope Paul VI reminded us that in the Church's liturgy Mary "is seen represented as a voice of praise, in unison with which the Church wishes to give glory to God: 'With Mary may we praise you forever' (Opening Prayer, Feast of the Visitation)."[9] Since St. Luke

31

presents Mary as a type or symbol of the Church praising God, the Church in her liturgy justly calls upon all peoples to join with Mary, the great voice of praise. Therefore in the second preface for feasts of Mary, we praise God by saying: "We do well always and everywhere to tell of your glory that your saints show forth, and especially as we celebrate the memory of the Blessed Virgin Mary. It is our special joy to glorify your love for us as we echo her song of thanksgiving." The rest of the preface clearly echoes the words of Mary's Magnificat: "What wonders you have worked throughout the world. All generations have shared the greatness of your love. When you looked on Mary your lowly servant, you raised her to be the mother of Jesus Christ your Son, our Lord, the savior of all mankind."

Alleluia!

The symphony of praise which began with Mary's greeting of Elizabeth will never stop till its crescendo has reached its eternal fullness in the liturgy of heaven:

> After this I heard what sounded like the loud song of a great assembly in heaven. They were singing, "Alleluia! Salvation, glory and might belong to our God, for his judgments are true and just!" Then I heard what sounded like the shouts of a great crowd, or the roaring of the deep, or mighty peals of thunder, as they cried, "Alleluia! The Lord is king, our God, the Almighty! Let us rejoice and be glad, and give him glory! For this is the wedding day of the Lamb; his bride has prepared herself for the wedding..." (Rev. 19:1-2, 6-7n).

The Book of Revelation resounds throughout with the praise of God for the victory which his suffering people are winning by the power of the risen Lamb (e.g.,12: 10-12).

Jesus sums it all up in Luke's Gospel, saying, "Rejoice that your names are inscribed in heaven" (Luke 10:20n). Rejoice that the Father has revealed himself to you, the little ones, who are enrolled in the family register of God's children (Luke 10:21-22). But Jesus' personal thrill of joy in the Holy Spirit goes even more deeply into the heart of the matter. To this we now turn. It is the Lord's own festal shout.

CHAPTER FOUR

"Jesus Thrilled with Joy"

Luke's Gospel of joyous praise has a little scene in which Jesus thrills with joy in the Holy Spirit and praises his heavenly Father. "Filled with joy by the Holy Spirit, he said, 'I bless you, Father, Lord of heaven and earth'" (10:21*j*).

The setting for this incident is significant. "The seventy-two came back rejoicing. 'Lord,' they said, 'even the devils submit to us when we use your name'" (10:17*j*).

Yes, Jesus admits, that is a cause for joy. He has given them power to tread underfoot all the power of the enemy (10:19). But great as is this motive for rejoicing, Jesus points out an even more wonderful reason for jubilation: "Yet do not rejoice that the spirits submit to you, rejoice rather that your names are written in heaven!" (10:20*j*). Rejoice not simply because you share in my power over evil, rejoice even more because you are enrolled as sons and daughters of God in the heavenly family register! The Lord's kingdom is not simply the defeat of the enemy. It is a marvelous positive gift of divine life! Do not harp on the devil. Give your full attention to your heavenly Father.

"It was *then* that Jesus thrilled with joy in the Holy Spirit and said, 'I bless you, Father, Lord of heaven and earth, for hiding these things from the learned and the clever and revealing them to mere children. Yes, Father, for that is what it pleased you to do" (10:21*b*). Christ's thrill of joy in the Spirit bursts forth at the thought that his disciples have been listed as God's children: he is overjoyed that the Father has revealed himself to them as their Father. The grace of adoption as sons and daughters of God is a grace of revelation of the Father.

Jesus thrills with joy because the Father has entrusted to him the work of revealing the Father, the work of bringing us into his own joy in the Father: "Everything has been entrusted to me by my Father" (10:22*j*). "Entrusted" (*paradidonai*) is a technical term in the Scriptures for the transmission of doctrine and divine revelation (e.g., 1 Cor.15:13). Jesus has been given the mission to reveal something which no one knows but the Father and he, a knowledge in which he shares fully with the Father. "No one knows who the Son is except the Father, and who the Father is except the Son, and those to whom the Son chooses to reveal him" (10:22*j*).

Thus, Jesus has power to reveal the inner divine life, the power to take his humble disciples into his very own knowledge of the Father, and thus share in his own divine sonship. Jesus chooses to do this; he thrills with joy over the privilege of doing it; he is overjoyed that his disciples share in his own joy in the Father; he rejoices that the Father is glorified in this way. "I have glorified you on earth. . . . I have made known your name to the men you took from the world to give me" (John 17: 4-6*j*). "Father, glorify your name!" (John 12:28*j*).

Thus, in the joy of Jesus we see the supreme reason

for jubilation. Jubilation is a thrill of joy in knowing the Father, it is joy that God is what he is: a loving Father who rejoices in his beloved Son, and in all whom he adopts as his children in the Son. We share in the Lord's own thrill of joy in the Holy Spirit: "The living waters within me cry, 'Hasten to the Father'" (St. Ignatius Martyr).

CHAPTER FIVE

St. Augustine on Jubilation

In his commentaries on the psalms, St. Augustine speaks so frequently and so warmly of jubilation that we can only conclude that he often experienced it deeply. Jubilation, according to Augustine, expresses in inarticulate sounds an unutterable, but irrepressible joy. It results from an experience of the inexpressible mystery of God. Man finds his most profound joy when he enters into this mystery in love. Anything less than God, says Augustine, is not really worthy of jubilation. But let us hear Augustine's own words on these matters.

> What is jubilation? Joy that cannot be expressed in words. Yet the voice expresses what is conceived in the heart and cannot be explained in words. This is jubilation. (On Ps.95:3)

> He who jubilates utters not words, but a wordless sound of joy. The voice of his heart pours forth joy as intensely as possible, expressing its affection in the best way it can, without reflection on any particular thought. To manifest his joy, the man does not use words that can be pronounced or

understood, but bursts forth into sounds of exaltation without words. It seems that he indeed rejoices with his voice, but with a joy so intense that he cannot express in words the subject of that joy. (On Ps.99:4)[10]

Augustine's comments seem to be a perfect description of praying in tongues and "singing in the Spirit," as these are experienced in contemporary charismatic communities.

To make clear that the overflowing joy resulting from the experience of God in love is the only jubilation fully worthy of the name, Augustine compares and contrasts it with a natural human jubilation, such as that experienced by reapers and vintagers. Commenting on Psalm 33:3, "Sing well to him with a loud noise (*teruwah, jubilatio*)," he writes:

Singing well to God means, in fact, just this: singing to him in jubilation. What does singing in jubilation mean? It is to experience that words cannot communicate the song of the heart. Just so, singers in the harvest or at vintage or in some other fervent work, delighted with the abundant produce, and rejoicing in the very richness and exuberance of the soil, sing in exultation. They express their rapture at first in songs set to words; then, as if bursting with a joy so full that they cannot express it in set words, they abandon words and break into the free melody of pure jubilation. (On Ps.32)[11]

Thus, there is a natural human jubilation, expressing the sheer joy of living. Augustine has observed this in the agricultural workers of his time, who enjoyed their work and their human companionship, and whose joy seemed to be an overflowing of the exuberant fruitfulness of the earth.

But Augustine has also experienced a divine jubilation, a rejoicing in God directly, an experiencing of God's own joy in his heart. This, he tells us, is the only jubilation fully worthy of the name:

> And to whom does jubilation rightly ascend if not to God the ineffable? Truly, he is the inexpressible One whom you cannot tell forth in speech. And if you cannot tell him forth in speech, yet ought not to remain silent, what else can you do but jubilate? In this, the heart rejoices without words, and the greatness of your joy without measure surpasses the limits of syllables. "Sing well to him in jubilation." (On Ps.32:3)[12]

Jubilation And Human Exhilaration

This divine jubilation is our theme, and we must not confuse it with merely human festal exhilaration. Even in a fervent Christian assembly, where the majority of those praising God may be experiencing a divine joy, there are probably always some whose joy is still only on the human level. This human joy of fellowship and celebration is a great good in itself, but is still an infinite distance from the divine jubilation of which we are speaking. The joy of Christian fellowship is at its peak only when Christians are rejoicing precisely in their experience of the Lord's own presence among them. Jubilation should not be content with any motive less than the experience of God himself. Therefore, Augustine speaks of the only jubilation fully worthy of the name:

> Jubilate for the Lord! Do not divide your jubilation among other things. All other things can somehow be expressed. God alone is inexpressible! (On Ps. 99)[13]

For the lesser joys, Augustine uses other words such as "exultation," reserving "jubilation" for the joy found in the direct experience of God himself. The only adequate motive for such jubilation is the grace of God in which we experience God himself in love. Augustine tells us this in his commentary on the words of Psalm 89, "Blessed are the people who know the festal shout" (Ps.89:15). The psalm opens with the words, "I will sing forever of your steadfast love, O Lord," and extols God's gift of himself to his people in covenant love. Augustine comments:

> In all these things shall we not rejoice? Shall we contain our joy? Shall words suffice for our gladness? Shall the tongue be able to express our rejoicing? Since therefore no words suffice, "blessed are the people who know glad shouting." For unless you understand glad shouting, you cannot be blessed. What do I mean by understanding glad shouting? I mean understanding the source of that rejoicing which is beyond words to express. For this joy is not of yourself, since "he that glories, let him glory in the Lord" (1 Cor.1:31). Rejoice then not in your own pride, but in God's grace. When you

40

realize that his grace is such that the tongue fails to express its greatness, you understand glad shouting. (On Ps.88)[14]

Jubilation and the Lesser Divine Joys

Augustine brings this out again by speaking first of lesser forms of divine joy, the joy which comes from contemplating God in his creation, seeing him especially in his spiritual creation, men and angels. But this is only a beginning, a way leading to the ineffable joy of jubilation in God as he is in himself. Commenting on Psalm 26:6, Augustine writes:

"I have gone round and have offered in his tabernacle a sacrifice of jubilation." We offer up a sacrifice of jubilation, we offer up a sacrifice of gladness, a sacrifice of rejoicing, a sacrifice of thanksgiving, which no words can express. But where do we offer it? In his own tabernacle, that is, in the Holy Church. And what is the sacrifice we offer? An overflowing and ineffable joy, beyond words, not to be expressed in speech. Such is the sacrifice of jubilation. Where seek for it, how find it? By looking everywhere. "I have gone round," says the psalmist, "and have offered in his tabernacle a sacrifice of jubilation." Let your mind roam round the whole creation; everywhere the created world will cry out to you, "God made me." Whatever pleases you in a work of art brings to mind the artist who wrought it; much more when you survey the universe does the consideration of it evoke praise for

41

its Maker. You look on the heavens; they are God's great work. You behold the earth; God made its numbers of seeds, its varieties of plants, its multitude of animals. Go around the heavens, and back again to earth, leave out nothing; on all sides everything cries out to you of its Author. Nay, the very forms of created things are, as it were, the voices with which they praise their Creator.

But who can fathom the whole creation? Who shall set forth its praises? Who shall worthily praise heaven and earth, the sea, and all things that are in them? And these indeed are visible things. Who shall worthily praise the angels, thrones, dominations, principalities and powers? Who shall worthily praise that power which works actively within ourselves, quickening the body, giving movement to the members, bringing the senses into play, embracing so many things in the memory, distinguishing so many things by the intelligence; who can worthily praise it?

Now if in considering these creatures of God human language is so at a loss, what is it to do in regard to the Creator? When words fail, can aught but triumphant music remain? "I have gone round and offered in his tabernacle a sacrifice of jubilation." (On Ps.26)[15]

Augustine repeats the same ideas in his commentary on Psalm 100, "Jubilate Deo Omnis Terra." Again, he speaks of the lesser exultation found in the consideration of God's creation. Then he concentrates on the wonders of his own spiritual being, which is called to experience the ineffable God himself, in spite of his dissimilarity with God. But in the instant that, in love, he surmounts this dissimilarity, and, in love, experiences God, he knows that God is, and arrives at last at true jubilation; for only then does he experience the truly inexpressible:

> When are we jubilant? When we praise that which cannot be uttered.... I have observed the bodily creation in heaven and on earth, and the spiritual in myself who am speaking.... The vision of God is promised to the human heart, and a certain purifying of the heart is enjoined in the Scriptures. Though called to see God, man is unlike God until he achieves purity of heart and true love of God.
>
> When you have become like him and have begun to approach and experience God, when love increases in you (since God is love) you will perceive what you were trying to say, and yet could not say. Before you experienced God in love, you thought that you could express God in words. You begin to experience him in the union of love, and at once you experience that you cannot speak what you experience.
>
> But when you have thus found that what you experience cannot be expressed, will you be mute, will you not praise God? Will you then be silent in the praises of God? Will you not offer up thanksgivings to him who has willed to make himself known to you? You praised him when you were seeking, will you be silent when you have found him? By no means! It is then that the jubilation which is fully worthy of the name bursts forth! (On Ps.99)[16]

CHAPTER SIX

Augustine's Jubilation in the Body of Christ

Augustine's ineffable God is not some vague, faceless "ground of being," but an intensely personal God, whom Augustine knows in an intimate personal relationship. He experiences this God only in Jesus Christ, and in his Body, the Church:

> I set about finding a way to gain the strength that was necessary for enjoying You. And I could not find it until I embraced the Mediator between God and man, the man Jesus Christ, "who is over all things, God blessed forever," who was calling me and saying, "I am the Way and the Truth and the Life," and who brought into union with our nature that Food which I lacked the strength to take: for the Word was made flesh that your Wisdom, by which you created all things, might give suck to our souls' infancy.[17]

Like Saints Paul and Athanasius before him, Augustine

44

receives the grace of jubilation only in the risen Lord. Jubilation is a response to the redemption and glory given to us in Jesus. In Jesus, he enjoys the ineffable God.

Jubilation In The Mystical Body

Augustine tells also how he has experienced jubilation in conscious union with the whole Body of Christ, the Church. He is always very much aware of what he loves to call "The Whole Christ," namely, the Mystical Body of Christ, the Church, God's people who are members of their Head, the risen Lord.

The reason for jubilation is the divine life and salvation granted to us in the victory of the risen Lord; but this life and salvation is experienced and celebrated in the Body of Christ, the Church. We are not content to jubilate alone; we invite the whole earth and all its inhabitants to rejoice with us; for we experience our communion with God in communion with the whole Body of the Lord. "Jubilate Deo omnis terra"—"Shout with joy to God, all the earth!" (Ps.66:1). Commenting on this "Psalm of the Resurrection," Augustine writes:

> Be joyful in God in every land. Let no one jubilate only in a part of the earth, let every land be joyful, let the catholic (universal) church jubilate! The catholic church embraces the whole earth. Whoever holds apart and is cut off from the whole, should howl, and not jubilate. (On Ps.65)[18]

45

Thus, jubilation expresses joy in the God whom we all possess together in the one Body of the Risen Lord. Many contemporary charismatic communities, like St. Augustine, are experiencing the festal shout as a call to ecumenism, and to the perfect reunion of the Body of Christ.

Jubilation, Augustine tells us, celebrates the victory which our Head, the risen Lord, shares with his members throughout the whole world:

> "I have gone around and offered in his tabernacle a sacrifice of jubilation." Since the psalmist has just told us (Ps.27:6), that he has been set up on the rock which is Christ, and that Christ his Head has been exalted above his enemies, he would thus have us understand that he himself, set up on the rock, has been raised up in the person of his Head beyond the reach of his enemies.
>
> Hereby he alludes to the glory of the Church, before which its persecutors have had to yield the victory; and because this victory has been achieved throughout the world by faith, I have gone round, the psalmist declares, and have offered in his tabernacle a sacrifice of jubilation. I have pondered on the faith of the whole world, this faith which exalts my Head above my persecutors, and in that tabernacle of his, that is, in the Church which embraces the whole world, I have praised the Lord in a way no words can tell. (On Ps.26:13)[19]

Thus, in Jesus Christ, and in communion with his Body, his people, Augustine experiences and rejoices in his God.

"I have gone round and have offered in his tabernacle a sacrifice of jubilation." I have considered
the whole round world believing in Christ, and
because God was humbled for our sakes in this
temporal order, I have praised him with rejoicing;
for with such sacrifice he is well pleased. "I will
sing and give praise to the Lord." Heart and deed
shall witness to my joy in the Lord. (On Ps.26:6)[20]

Jubilation In Hippo

Besides his joy in the whole Church throughout the
world, St. Augustine has also witnessed and taken part in
the intense jubilation of his local Church, the flock
which he shepherded as Bishop of Hippo. He describes
two such outbursts of jubilation on occasions when the
whole assembly experienced the presence and power of
the risen Lord working in their midst, granting miraculous healings of the sick. When a young man named
Paulus was completely healed of disease, and stood
before the congregation assembled for the Easter Eucharist, "everyone," says Augustine, "burst into a prayer of
thankfulness to God. The whole church soon rang with
the clamor of rejoicing. . . . In the crowded church, cries
of joy rose up everywhere, 'Thanks be to God!' 'Praise
be to God!' with everyone joining and shouting on all
sides, 'I have healed the people,' and then with still
louder voices shouting again."[21]

The next day the young man's sister, Palladia, was also
healed of the disease, and again "the tumult of joy"
burst forth:

47

Such wonder rose from men and women together, that the exclamations and the tears seemed as if they would never come to an end. . . . They shouted God's praises without words, but with such a noise that our ears could scarcely bear it. What was there in the hearts of all this clamoring crowd but the faith of Christ, for which St. Stephen shed his blood?[22]

Thus, Augustine attributes the jubilation to their experience of Christ *in faith*. On this occasion, it is a response to the power of the risen Lord working in the assembly of his people. These events took place at Eastertime, when the people were assembled for the Eucharist, and the healings were granted through the intercession of St. Stephen, the first martyr; for the two people were praying at St. Stephen's shrine when they were healed. They had come to Africa all the way from Asia Minor to seek the intercession of St. Stephen.

Therefore, Augustine points out the relationship of these miracles, and of many others which he had witnessed, with the sacraments of the Church, and with the whole communion of saints—not only God's people assembled on earth, but even the saints already with God in glory.

Augustine, we said, was always conscious of the whole Christ, the whole communion of saints, whether newly baptized or already in heaven because they have been baptized in the blood of martyrdom. Any wonders God works in his people here and now are but the continuation of the wonders of the paschal mystery of Jesus, the death and resurrection of the Lord.

At first, miracles were widely known so as to awaken people's faith, but now they are becoming even more widely known because of the faith they have in fact awakened. . . . And today miracles still go on happening in our Lord's name, through the sacraments he instituted, and through the prayers and memoriae of his saints.[23]

One of his favorite expressions was "we are all one body under one Head." The risen Lord continues his works of power not only through the intercession and witness of his saints and martyrs, members of his Body who are now in glory, but even through the newly baptized, the newest members of his Body, those who have died and risen with Jesus in baptism. Augustine relates that a woman suffering from breast cancer was told in a dream to go to the baptistry at Easter and ask the first woman who emerged from the baptismal waters to make a sign of the cross over the cancer. She did this and was healed, to the astonishment of her doctor.[24]

Thus, we see that Christian praise is a response in faith to the presence and power of the risen Lord working in the Body, which is his people, the people who are the communion of saints, whether on earth or with God in glory. Many contemporary charismatic communities are experiencing precisely these realities. We shall reserve their witness till later, however, for it illustrates other points which we have not yet made.

Augustine's Interior Jubilation

Although for Augustine jubilation has sometimes been

49

a group experience of loud, wordless praise at the top of the voice, shared with the people of his flock, he has also experienced a silent interior praise:

> My confession of praise is not by bodily words or bodily cries, but with words of the soul and the upward cry of my thought, which your ear knows, O Lord. . . . And so my confession in your sight is made silently; and yet not silently, for it it makes no sound, yet it cries aloud in my heart.[25]

Many contemporary charismatics also tell of an intense clamor of praise in the heart, which does not necessarily break forth into sound. St. Gregory the Great (died 604), too, accentuates the distinction between interior jubilation and the jubilation expressed in sound. "Jubilus is unspeakable joy conceived in the heart, which can neither be hidden nor expressed in words. . . . Hence, often from the jubilus of the heart there bursts forth the jubilus of vociferation."[26]

A member of the charismatic Christian Community of God's Delight tells of her intense longing for silence and solitude even when she is in the midst of the praising community. When she first "came into the Lord," loud praise along with the community was her most delightful way of praising God. But the gift of praise began to develop in her heart in an ever more interior way. One Sunday when the presence of the Lord was even more powerfully manifest than usual in the praises of the community, she experienced a profound longing to be alone with the Lord in silence and solitude.

This worried her a bit, for loud praise is so strongly emphasized in her community that those who long for silence sometimes feel a bit guilty. The next day she came to me asking whether it was right for her to desire solitude when the Lord was obviously present in the midst of the loud community praise. I assured her that, far from being wrong, this was a normal development of the gift of God's loving presence. An indication of this is the fact that a community's singing in the Spirit is always followed by at least some moments of deep silence in the Lord's presence. The Spirit himself suddenly cuts off the singing and his presence is felt in silent awe. People should learn to savor this presence in silent attentiveness. Many a charismatic deeply regrets, and justly so, that his praising community does not take care to prolong these periods of silence, which for some are a God-given gift of interior silence. Silent adoration of the Lord in the simplicity of complete openness to his love can be a high form of praise, for it is recognition and appreciation of his more interior gifts of infused contemplation.

Interior praise is the fruit of vocal praise. A business man, a leader in our charismatic community says, "When I praise aloud with the community, I find that I am more and more drawn within myself to interior praise. Interior praise becomes an experience of the very presence of God in my heart."

Thus, while there is a time for expressing externally with a joyful noise and with dance the irrepressible joy of the heart, there is a time also for interior silent awe and attentiveness to the interior Word of grace. This interior Word is the very presence of the Son of God, the Word who enlightens interiorly by his presence in the heart.

If singing and loud praise can prepare the heart for

this interior presence, when the preparation is complete, it must give way to the God-given grace of silence of the heart, a silence which is the effect of his presence.

Perhaps St. Augustine is referring to this inner silence, when, in the same commentary in which he speaks so eloquently of loud praise, he adds a little later: "Come before his presence with rejoicing. It is easy to rejoice outwardly. Rejoice before the presence of God. Let not the tongue be too joyful, let the interior consciousness be joyful" (Ps.100:10).[27] Perhaps in these words Augustine is simply warning against mere outward praise without the inner praise of the heart. But he knows, too, of the totally interior praise in the silence of the heart. Because of this inner, God-given silence caused by his very presence, the joyful tongue must sometimes become still. Even earthly lovers know that there are times when silence filled with each other's presence is far more eloquent than words and songs of love.

PART TWO

Praise: Response to God's Word

CHAPTER SEVEN

Praise: Response to God's Word

St. Jerome tells us that the psalms are the entire revelation of God expressed in the form of praise. They are the divinely inspired response of man to God's self-revelation. Hence they are an invaluable source of prayer. God has revealed himself both in word and in his works of salvation. And by his self-revelation he has inspired in the hearts of men the faith and hope and love, the sorrow for sin and the repentance, the thanksgiving and joy and praise which are expressed in the psalms.

As response to God's self-revelation, the psalms themselves are revelation of God. God, to whom the psalmist responds, is revealed in the very response. For we get some idea of what God himself must be like when the inspired poets can turn to him with such confidence, such faith and love, such contrition and reparation, such joy and thanksgiving, such fullness of praise. He who inspires such total trust in these men who knew him so well must be completely faithful and trustworthy. He who inspires such reverence and adoration and contrition must be majestic and holy. He who draws forth from human hearts such praise and loving thanksgiving must be all good and loving. The psalms are the witness of a people who really knew God.

But more than that, since the psalms are God's own inspired word to us, when we use them with reverent faith God speaks through them directly to our heart. He reveals himself to us here and now as we use them, so that they draw forth from us a response as authentic as that originally expressed by their inspired composers. For like all the Sacred Scriptures, the psalms were not only originally inspired by the Holy Spirit, but in them the Holy Spirit continues here and now to speak to men of reverent faith.

Thus, in the psalms God himself teaches us how to pray, how to respond both to what he has done for his people in the past and to what he is doing now for each of us.

The more familiar one is with the entire revelation of God to which the psalms are a response, the better one can respond to God in their use. Growing familiarity with the rest of the scriptures brings growing familiarity with the deeper meaning of the psalms and greater facility in using them to express our own response to what God is doing for us here and now. For though the psalms were composed in response to God's self-revelation in past salvation history, we use them in response to his self-giving in the present continuation of that history.

We can use the psalms well, in other words, only in the light of the whole of salvation history as begun in the Old Testament, as continued in the New Testament, and as here and now being completed in each of us by Jesus Christ. The God revealed in the psalms was faithful and steadfast in love toward the people whose poets composed the psalms; he was faithful and steadfast in love towards Jesus and towards Paul who prayed the psalms; and Paul, quoting the psalms, shows that this God is merciful and loving toward the people of all nations (Rom. 15:4-13).

To pray the psalms, we must see that God is all of this for us, just as he was all of this for the people of Israel, and for Jesus and his disciples. God is everything for us that he was for them, because we are indeed one people with the chosen people of old. We must pray the psalms in true solidarity with that people, and we must pray the psalms in tune with our own times. These divinely inspired prayers do fit the situations of all times, for they express the relationships with God which are valid in every age.

We pray the psalms as one with God's people especially when we use them in the liturgy of the Eucharistic celebration and in the liturgy of the hours. For liturgy is the prayer of the whole people of God. The psalms, we said, are the inspired response to God's salvation deeds. These deeds are still in process of being accomplished in us. And that is how the Church uses the psalms in the liturgy. For example, each day in the Eucharistic celebration, the response to the first reading in the liturgy of the word is always a psalm which responds explicitly to the point of the reading. In the first reading on Wednesday of the Twenty-Second Week of the Year, for example, St. Paul gives thanks for the wonderful fruits of the preaching of the Gospel among the Colossians. We respond in a psalm in which we too give thanks, and tell of God's wonderful works accomplished in us.

Salvation History Continued

The Bible itself teaches us how to respond to salvation history and live it here and now, how to become personally involved in God's self-communication, which was begun in Abraham and Moses, brought to perfection in Christ, and is being continued by Christ in us now, in our day, especially through the Eucharistic liturgy.

The book of Deuteronomy gives us a clue how to do this in its description of the liturgy of the offering of the first fruits (Deut.26:1-11). What is true of this liturgy of the first fruits is true of all Jewish and Christian liturgy. Liturgy is always a ceremony, and the words accompanying the ceremonial actions give deeper meaning to the ceremony. The words and ceremony are a profession of faith. By this profession, the worshipper identifies himself with the original mystery of faith which he is celebrating. In this case of the first fruits, the mystery of the Exodus from Egypt and the passing into the promised land is being celebrated. The first fruits of the land are a most fitting offering in thanksgiving for being brought out of slavery into the land which God had promised to Father Abraham.

The worshipper identifies himself with the people involved in the original mystery. He is one with that people, and with them he participates in one same salvation. His words of offering show that it is as though he personally had gone forth from Egypt with his people many centuries before: "When the Egyptians maltreated and oppressed *us* ... *we* cried to the Lord, the God of our Fathers.... He brought *us* out of Egypt with his strong hand and outstretched arm ... and bringing *us* into this country, he gave us this land flowing with milk and honey" (Deut.26:6-9n).

Thus, the worshipping community of the here and now professes its faith in its identity with the community which was saved in the Exodus. It is not a different community, it is one same people.

By this identification in faith with the original mystery of salvation which he is celebrating, the worshipper actually enters into that same salvation as here and now being continued. He becomes personally involved in the ever-present salvation which God is still bringing about in his people.

Thus, in this particular liturgy of the first fruits, the man making the offering sees that the first fruits of the harvest which God has given him are but the continuation of what God accomplished for his people in giving them the promised land which bore the fruits. At the same time, the first fruits are a promise of continuing favors from God in the years to come. These first fruits of the earth are a symbol and pledge of all the fruits of salvation.

Thus, the community worship is an act of *faith* in the same God who in all generations is forever faithful to his covenant with his people. It is an act of *hope* in the same covenant promises made in the distant past, a sharing in hope for the continuing benefits of the covenant. It is an act of *love* in response to the steadfast love of God who keeps his covenant. It is a true receiving of the benefits of salvation in this openness of faith, hope, and love. It is a thanksgiving not only for the past and for the present but also for the future, for God is saving one people, in eternal faithfulness to his promises. The future is certain because of God's steadfast love, and praise and thanksgiving for the benefits to come are already in order, because he is our faithful God.

The New Song

This idea of ever-renewed, ever-continuing salvation is expressed in the theme of the "new song" so prevalent in the Bible. The "old song" was the canticle of Moses after the crossing of the Red Sea (Exod. 15). Each new salvation event called for a new song.

> Sing to the Lord a new song, for he has done wondrous deeds; His right hand has won victory for him, his holy arm. The Lord has made his salvation known: in the sight of the nations he has revealed his justice. He has remembered his kindness and his faithfulness toward the house of Israel. All the ends of the earth have seen the salvation by our God (Ps.98:1-3n).

But each new salvation event was seen as a continuation of God's justice: "in the sight of the nations he has revealed his justice" (Ps.98:2n), "his just deeds that brought freedom to Israel" (Judg.5:11n). His saving deeds are "just deeds" because they are the expression of God's faithfulness to his covenant and promises. It is "just" for God to save his people, even when his people have been unfaithful, for their unfaithfulness does not cancel his faithfulness. He cannot deny himself, he works justice by being true to himself and to his promises to save his people.

Because of his endless saving deeds, Israel became "the

60

people whom I formed for myself that they might announce my praise" (Isa.43:21n), and thus witness to God's love before all the nations: "You are my witnesses, says the Lord, my servants whom I have chosen" (Isa. 43:10n). They are the people who are ever singing a new song of praise for his just deeds of salvation.

In Deutero-Isaiah, the prophet tells us that God will perform greater deeds of salvation than ever before. His deeds of the past will seem like nothing in contrast (Isa.43:18-19). There will be a new exodus surpassing in greatness the old exodus from Egypt, and so a new song will be sung (Isa.42:10). Thus Israel's liturgy was even more an expression of hope for the future than of thanksgiving for the past, for God is ever faithful to his promises, and can be thanked even in advance.

The hope expressed in Old Testament liturgy was fulfilled in Christ, who is the "Yes" to all of God's promises (2 Cor.1:20). Though Deutero-Isaiah was thinking of the return from Babylon as the new exodus, his prophecy was more wonderfully fulfilled in our redemption by Jesus Christ, in his exodus from this world to the Father (John 13:1). It was of this new exodus that Jesus spoke in his conversation with Moses and Elijah at the Transfiguration (Luke 9:31).

And hence we sing the new song of praise and thanksgiving for our redemption in Christ. To do this, we use not only Our Lady's song, the Magnificat (Luke 1:46-55), but all psalms and canticles of the Old and New Testament in which we express praise and thanks.

Even the "old song" of Moses is used to praise God for the new exodus in Christ. For example, on Tuesday of the Sixteenth Week of the Year, when the story of the crossing of the Red Sea (Exod.14) is read in the Eucharistic liturgy, it is a real thrill to respond to the story in the words of the song of Moses (Exod.15), for all of this is a vivid symbol of our salvation in Christ which we commemorate in each Eucharistic celebration.

Another example of the use of an Old Testament song to celebrate the New Testament salvation occurs in Sunday Evening Prayer. When we use the words of Psalm 111, "I will thank the Lord with all my heart ... great are the works of the Lord" (v.1-2n), we have in mind especially the work of redemption accomplished by the death and resurrection of Jesus. "He has given food to those who fear him" (v.5n) is used as praise for the gift of the Eucharist. "He will be forever mindful of his covenant" (v.5n) expresses confidence in his faithfulness to the new and eternal covenant sealed in the Blood of Jesus.

For the salvation granted in Christ is still in the process of being accomplished in us today, who are one people with those who were present with Jesus at the Last Supper when he blessed the cup and passed it around to his disciples, saying, "This cup is the new covenant in my blood, which will be shed for you" (Luke 22:20). Our participation in the Eucharistic liturgy in faith is a sharing in this on-going work of salvation; and in evening prayer we express our continuing praise and thanksgiving in words like those of Psalm 111.

Since all the psalms and canticles in the Scriptures are the songs of a whole people, each and every one of them—no matter how personal and individual its sentiments may seem to be—is an act of faith by which we participate in the salvation of the whole people. There is a psalm for every situation. Each psalm is a symbol of some aspect or other of God's saving work, and can be used to praise him for his saving deeds as continued in us.

Each favor granted or petitioned, no matter how small it is in itself, is seen as an expression of God's steadfast love and ever-continuing faithfulness to his covenant with us. The recovery granted to a sick person in our days is as much a continuation of Christ's saving work as the gift of the harvest was a continuation of the saving work of the Exodus and the giving of the promised land. Thus, in Psalm 40, when God rescues a sick man from the brink of death, the man sings a new song and gives praise to God in the assembly of the whole people, for his recovery is a participation in the salvation of the whole people:

> I have waited, waited for the Lord,
> and he stooped toward me and heard my cry.
> He drew me out of the pit of destruction,
> out of the mud of the swamp. . . .
> And he put a new song into my mouth,
> a hymn to our God.
> Many shall look on in awe
> and trust in the Lord. . . .
> I announced your justice in the vast assembly . . .
> your faithfulness and your salvation I have spoken of.
> (Ps.40:2-4, 10-11n)

God's covenant qualties, "steadfast love and faithfulness," are celebrated repeatedly in the psalms. It is well to note this, for these are his qualities also in the new and eternal covenant, which we celebrate when we use the psalms of the old covenant, putting this new content into the words. "Steadfast love and faithfulness" are variously translated as "kindness and fidelty," "mercy and justice," "mercy and truth," "love and faithfulness," etc. When we notice these words in the psalms, we respond with praise of God and trust in his covenant love.

CHAPTER EIGHT

Recognize Christ's Voice in You

In praying the psalms, we express not only our solidarity with the whole redeemed covenant people of God, but above all our solidarity with Jesus himself.

Jesus prayed the psalms because he was one with his people. He was born of them and into their midst. They were the prayers of his people, and he prayed them with them.

But more than that, he prayed them for them. Everything he did was for them (and by "them" we mean God's people in every century both B.C. and A.D.). In becoming like his people in all things but sin, he truly suffered with them and for them. "It was our infirmities that he bore, our sufferings that he endured" (Isa. 53:4n). He accepted as his own his people's anguish, their needs, their joys, and he cried out in their sufferings which he had truly made his own. He cried out in their very own words of anguish, using one of their psalms as he hung on the cross, "My God, my God, why have you forsaken me" (Ps. 22:2; Matt. 27:46n), showing that he was truly one with them.

Hence St. Augustine's famous words: "Recognize your voice in Christ's"—it is your cry of anguish, your sinfulness, your neediness which he expresses as he prays the psalms—"and recognize his voice in you." For now that he has become one with all suffering mankind, taking our sufferings and our sinfulness and our cry as his own, he cries out in each one of us when we cry out, and for each one of us. As the fruit of his suffering for and with us, his own Holy Spirit is in us and forms his own cry in us, so that through him and with him and in him we too say, "Father, into your hands I commend my spirit" (Ps.31:6; Luke 23:46n).

One example of how the Old Testament psalms can be used to express our New Testament faith is Psalm 21. This is a psalm of thanksgiving that the king's prayers have been answered. But when we pray it, the King we think of is Jesus, who expressed his heart's desire in the prayer at the Last Supper. "You have granted him his heart's desire; you refused not the wish of his lips. For you welcomed him with godly blessings" (Ps. 21:3-4n).

In the old liturgy for the Vigil of the Ascension, the Gospel reading was Christ's prayer at the Last Supper (John 17). Jesus expressed "his heart's desire" in that prayer, which was his prayer for all of us. And his cries on the cross expressed the profound neediness of every one of us, for he was one with us all. All of these prayers of Jesus have been answered in his Ascension into heaven. And therefore on the Feast of the Ascension we sang Psalm 21: "You have granted him his heart's desire. . . . He asked life of you; you gave him length of days forever and ever" (Ps. 21:3,5n). When we pray that particular psalm, we are joyous in the conviction that all our prayers are heard in Christ, whose prayer was heard.

Jesus was able to give thanks even before he asked for anything: "Father, I thank you for having heard me; I know that you always hear me" (John 11:41-42n). These were his words of thanksgiving for the raising of Lazarus even before he called him from the tomb, so certain was he that he would be heard. We too give thanks even before we ask, and while we ask, knowing that in Jesus our prayer is heard.

The Ministry of Prayer

We enter into the prayer of Jesus which has been heard by the Father and we make it our own. Thus our cry will be heard in him, for we pray only through Jesus Christ our Lord.

We offer in his prayer not just our personal prayer, and not just the prayers of our friends and acquaintances. We offer the prayers of all God's people, and indeed, the prayers of all mankind. For we are one with the whole human race not just in flesh and blood, but more marvelously so in our union with Christ our Head, who is the Head of all. We should pray the psalms in consciousness of this union with Jesus and with all our fellowmen, thus presenting the cries of all to the Father in Jesus.

Thus we carry out a ministry of prayer on behalf of all those for whom Christ died. In a special way, the official liturgy of the Church is a ministry of prayer, and when we pray the liturgy of the hours, we are one with all of God's people as ministers praying on their behalf and in their name. The liturgy of the hours (formerly known as the divine office) is the Church's official prayer of praise, in addition to the Eucharistic liturgy.

Vatican II urged all of God's people to join in this liturgy. We should at least unite ourselves in our hearts with Christ and all his people whenever we pray.

There is a psalm to fit every human need, every human situation. But suppose I am praying the psalms in the liturgy of the hours in the name of the whole Christian community. As minister of the community, I pray prescribed psalms. But what if these psalms do not fit my personal mood or my personal need? For example, I am sad, and I am given psalms of joy and praise. Or I am full of joy and thanksgiving, and I am given psalms of anguish and suffering. I am innocent of heart, and I am given psalms of sinfulness and contrition. Or I am deeply aware of my sinfulness, and I am given psalms of innocence.

What am I to do? Shall I reject the psalms assigned and choose my own? Not at all. Otherwise I would be serving myself, and not God's people. The psalms are the prayers of Christ, and therefore of all his members.

If the psalm is the cry of a sick man, a dying man, an old man, but I am a young woman, healthy and strong, then I recognize that man's voice is mine. I offer his neediness to the Lord in my prayer, for he and I are one body under our one Head Jesus. I recognize the man's cry here and now as taken up into the cry of anguish of Jesus on the cross and into my cry of prayer for him. I thus fulfill my ministry of love, strengthening the old man's prayer in my own, offering his prayer and mine in that of Jesus. I ask Jesus to draw our prayers into his own.

When I was a young man in my twenties, I noticed that Psalm 119 is the prayer of a young man: "How shall a young man be faultless in his ways? By keeping to your words. . . . I have more understanding than all my teachers when your decrees are my meditation. I have more discernment than the elders because I observe your precepts" (Ps. 119:9,99n). For more than thirty-five years I continued to pray this psalm of a young man with joy and profit, never realizing that I was growing older and older all the time.

Then one day a young brother in the Lord was giving me a haircut. He remarked, "My, but you have a lot of hair for an old man." Since that day I have relished more than ever another psalm, "Now that I am old and gray, O God, forsake me not!" (Ps.71:18n). But the other psalm had helped keep me young in heart, and so I still pray it with truth and relevancy, and, moreover, in solidarity with all the young people who are one with me in the Lord.

Praying with the whole community of God's people as their minister, praying as one with the whole Mystical Body of Christ, I am taken out of my narrowness and my heart is broadened in love. The psalms, as the prayers of a whole people, have a way of taking me out of myself and into Christ and his members. And yet there are plenty of psalms which express my most intimate personal needs. If I am faithful to the liturgical cycle of psalms and pray them all, I will come regularly to the ones I myself need most, and at the same time will be praying for and with all my needy fellowmen.

When we pray in the Eucharistic liturgy or in the liturgy of the hours, we give expression, in union with Jesus, to the prayers of all our suffering brothers and sisters in all of mankind. Our redemptive prayer in Christ is thus a continuation here and now of the redemptive prayer of Jesus on the cross. This is a wonderful ministry. Salvation is here and now being accomplished *in us* through our solidarity with God's people who are in the process of receiving Christ's redemption, but it is also being accomplished *through us* in others, because of our solidarity with the redeeming Christ in prayer for others. We offer the cries of his suffering members in union with Christ's cries on the cross. Their cries find expression in Christ through our cries for them. Such is the ministry of intercessory prayer.

CHAPTER NINE

Praising the God Who Is Near

Jubilation, we said, is joy that God is what he is. It celebrates what the Lord is in himself, more than what he does for us.

To this someone may object, saying that biblical man praised the Lord for his wonderful works, rather than for his inner life: "O give thanks to the Lord, call on his name, make known *his deeds* among the peoples! Sing to him, sing praises to him, tell of all *his wonderful works!*" (Ps.105:1-2). The Hebrew was a practical, down to earth man, and met his God in what God was doing in man's daily life. And the first Christians were no different. When they were filled with the Holy Spirit, it was said of them, "We hear them telling in our own tongues the mighty works of God" (Acts 2:11).

A closer look at the psalms shows, however, that in praising God's mighty deeds, his people were really praising his steadfast love and faithfulness to his covenant which produced these deeds. They were praising God himself who was expressing his covenant love in these wonderful works. In this love and in these works he was giving himself and manifesting his presence. Thus, Psalm

71

105 continues: "Glory in his holy name," that is, in his presence; for his Name, he himself, dwelt among his people. "Let the hearts of those who seek the Lord rejoice! Seek the Lord and his strength, seek *his presence* continually. Remember the wonderful works that he has done.... He is mindful of his covenant forever" (Ps. 105:3-8).

Psalm 9 sums it all up in one verse: "I will proclaim you, O Lord, with all my heart; I will declare all your wonderful deeds. I will be glad and exult *in you*; I will sing praise to your name, Most High" (Ps.9:1).

One does not praise an abstract God, the God of the philosophers, nor a distant, unconcerned God, the God of the deists. One praises only a God who has been experienced in joy, who has touched our lives by his presence, the living God who speaks to his people and communicates with them, who acts and manifests his presence in his marvelous deeds on their behalf. Such is the God of the Bible. All God's marvelous deeds in saving his people have as their purpose to gather this people to himself, that he might give himself to them in covenant love and communion.

Biblical man is not concerned only with what God does for him in nature and in history, he is concerned about personal communion with this loving God who manifests his presence in history and in nature. The sacrifices of thanksgiving which man offers to God are "peace offerings" which are for the sake of communion with him.[28] Life, for the Hebrew, is communion with the living God. To be cut off from this communion is death. The fullness of life is praise of God and rejoicing in him: "What profit is there in my death, if I go down to the Pit? Will the dust praise you? Will it tell of your faithfulness? . . . You have loosed my sackcloth and girded me with gladness, that my soul may praise and not be silent. O Lord, my God, I will praise you forever!" (Ps. 30: 9-12).

To praise the Lord for his marvelous deeds, then, is to praise him for his loving presence in steadfast love and faithfulness to his covenant. In their communion with the God who gives himself, his people taste of him (Ps. 34:8), and rejoice in *what he is* even more than in what he has done.

Thus we are told in Chronicles how the Lord manifested his presence when his people praised him and proclaimed his steadfast love. "When the trumpeters and singers were heard as a single voice praising and giving thanks to the Lord, and when they raised the sound of the trumpets, cymbals and other musical instruments to 'give thanks to the Lord, for he is good, for his mercy endures forever,' the building of the Lord's temple was filled with a cloud. The priests could not continue to minister because of the cloud, since the Lord's glory filled the house of God" (2 Chron. 5:13-14n).

The "Lord's glory" was a striking manifestation of God's presence and power. At this manifestation of his presence, the people repeated their song of praise: "All the Israelites looked on when the fire came down and the glory of the Lord was upon the house, and they fell down upon the pavement with their faces to the earth and adored, praising the Lord, 'for he is good, for his mercy endures forever' " (2 Chron.7:3n).

"The Sacrifice of Praise"

The title of the song used on this occasion, "Give

73

thanks (praise) to the Lord, for he is good, for his mercy endures forever," was a standard liturgical formula used with the *todah*, "the sacrifice of praise," which was a sacrificial meal of thanksgiving. When a person offered a thanksgiving sacrifice, he called his family and friends together to eat the sacrifice with him, and at the sacrifice he proclaimed before the whole assembly all the wonderful things God had done for him.[29]

The word *todah*, sacrifice of praise, is derived from the word *yadah*. The basic meaning of *yadah* is "to use (hold out) the hand." It came to mean "to revere, to worship," because the bread which was offered with the *todah*, the sacrifice of praise, was held on outstretched hands (Lev.7:12-13). It is easy to see how the *offering of self* is spontaneously expressed with outstretched hands: "Lift up your hands to the holy place, and bless the Lord!" (Ps.134:2).

No doubt long before there was such a thing as a *todah* liturgy, people already spontaneously raised their hands to acclaim the presence of the Lord, to praise him, thank him, to surrender self lovingly to his loving presence. This is what charismatics today usually express by their raised hands: the yielding of self completely to the Lord whose loving presence they acclaim.

Several psalms, undoubtedly composed for these thanksgiving sacrifices, begin with the words, "Give thanks (*yadah*) to the Lord, for he is good, for his steadfast love endures forever" (Ps. 106, 107, 118, 136). Some scholars have argued convincingly that the verb *yadah* used here, meaning "to hold out the hand" and usually translated "give thanks," should be rendered "proclaim the Lord" or "testify to the Lord, for he is good." The Douay translated it, "glorify the Lord."[30]

Yadah is usually translated "give thanks" because the formula was used in connection with the sacrifice of thanksgiving. However, an Israelite thanked God, we said, not only by saying, "Thank you, Lord," but by gathering his friends together at a sacrificial meal and praising the Lord before them by *proclaiming* the Lord's steadfast love and the wonderful deeds he had done in that love.

That is why the thanksgiving meal was called a "sacrifice of praise." Thanksgiving for individual personal favors from God was always presented in the context of praise for all his salvation deeds on behalf of the whole people; for the Lord's personal favors to an individual were but a continuation and manifestation of God's covenant love for all the people. The Christian Eucharist, also called "the Sacrifice of Praise" (Eucharistic Prayer I), is a sacrifice and a meal and a proclamation of God's presence and steadfast love as this love and presence have been brought to perfect fulfillment in the risen Lord Jesus.

Thus we see the deeper motive for celebrating the wonderful deeds of the Lord: these deeds are the manifestation of God's continuing presence with his people in faithfulness to his covenant of loving communion. They are the expression of his steadfast love and faithfulness, in which he is ever gathering a people to himself, who are called to live in deep communion with him.

Psalm 136, for example, opens with the words, "Proclaim the Lord, for he is good, for his steadfast love endures forever." This is followed by a long litany proclaiming the great wonders which the Lord has accomplished in his love for his people: his mighty works in creating and ruling the universe and in rescuing his people from their enemies in the course of history. Each statement in the litany is followed by the refrain, "for his steadfast love endures forever." In covenant love, God is in continuing communion with his people.

This psalm, 136, was called the Great Hallel, and was recited at the Passover meal after the Little Hallel (Psalms 113-18). The Passover meal is thus manifestly a "sacrifice of praise" in thanksgiving for the wonders of the Exodus and for God's continuing deeds for his people in faithful love. "Hallel" meant "to sing praises, to celebrate." The root meaning of the word is "to be clear, to shine forth." To proclaim the Lord because he is good is to make him clearly shine forth to others so that they too might praise him: Alleluia!

The principle element in the praise psalms, then, is publicly proclaiming what God has done, and *what he is*. For what he has done manifests what he is: the God of covenant love, who lives in communion with his people. In all that he is doing, he is giving of himself.

Many Words for Praise

Publicly proclaiming the Lord's covenant love was so important in Hebrew spirituality that many other words besides *yadah* and *hallel* were used to express this witnessing to God before others. So exuberant is the joy in the Lord and in his covenant love that one must tell it to others in as many ways as possible. The different words bring out different manners and circumstances for praising God.

Thus, there are times when boldness is necessary in this praise of the Lord. The word *nagad*, "to declare, to announce," in its root meaning signifies "to stand boldly opposite." It means to announce by word of mouth to one who is present: "Tell (*nagad*) among the peoples his deeds! For he who avenges blood is mindful of them; he does not forget the cry of the afflicted" (Ps. 9:11-12). God's vindicating justice must be boldly proclaimed in the face of oppression.

So manifold are God's favors that they have to be marked down, recorded, and celebrated. The word *caphar* (saw-far), "to *score* with a mark as a tally, to enumerate, to recount," came to mean "to celebrate, to publish." "O sing to the Lord a new song. . . . Declare (*caphar*) his glory among the nations, his marvelous works among the peoples. . . . Ascribe to the Lord the glory due his name" (Ps.96:1,3,8). Give him credit for what he has done! "Let them thank the Lord for his steadfast love . . . and tell (*caphar*) of his deeds in songs of joy" (Ps.107:21-22).

When the singer exults in God's love and protection, he uses the word *ranan*, "to shout out for joy, to triumph." "O my Strength, I will sing praises to you (*ranan*)"—I will extol you triumphantly—"for you, O God, are my fortress, the God who shows me steadfast love" (Ps.59:17).

All the glory, the honor, the credit, the attention is directed to the Lord himself. Praise is "weighted" towards God. the word *kabod*, meaning "to be heavy," came to mean "to be rich, honorable, highly endowed, to be glorious," and thence "to glorify, to honor." "I will *glorify* your name forever" (Ps.86:12). "Sing the glory of his name; give to him glorious praise!" (Ps. 66:1).

We can understand why the Lord is stirring up praise

in this world of the last half of the twentieth century, when his presence and love and power have been obscured by the wickedness and oppression and chaos of a collapsing world. In the evils of our times, God seems often to be the "absent," "silent," "hidden" God. The Lord's vindication of the downtrodden must be boldly declared, his rocklike presence with his downtrodden people must be proclaimed, his love which seems camouflaged by the evils of our times must be announced in unwavering faith. The glorious riches of his love and presence must be proclaimed to counteract the attraction of the deceitful riches and pleasures of the world.

The Voice of the Bridegroom

Jeremiah makes a beautiful reference to the sacrifice of praise. On an earlier page he had announced the doom of the land of Judah: "I will bring to an end the song of joy and the song of gladness, the voice of the bridegroom and the voice of the bride, the sound of the millstone and the light of the lamp" (Jer.25:10n). The whole land shall be desolate.

But later the prophet announces a reversal of the doom: "In this place . . . there shall yet be heard the cry of joy, and the cry of gladness, the voice of the bridegroom and the voice of the bride, the sound of those who bring the sacrifice of praise to the house of the Lord, singing, 'Praise the Lord of hosts, for the Lord is good, for his steadfast love endures forever!' " (Jer.33: 10-11n,k).

He is the same "Lord of hosts" who had been acclaimed by the Israel of old in the days of the holy wars. He is still winning victories for his people. His steadfast love is forever faithful!

John the Baptist, calling himself the friend of the Bridegroom, is referring to Jeremiah's prophecy when he says, "He who has the bride is the bridegroom; the friend of the bridegroom, who stands and hears him, rejoices greatly at *the bridegroom's voice*; therefore this joy of mine is now full" (John 3:29). The restoration announced by Jeremiah is accomplished by Jesus: "There shall yet be heard the cry of joy and the cry of gladness, the voice of the bridegroom and the voice of the bride!"

When the other John, in the Book of Revelation, tells of the destruction of "Babylon, the great city" (Rev. 18:21), the symbol of the world organized in sin against God, he echoes again Jeremiah's words of doom, addressing them this time to those who have rejected Christ. He makes them even more intense and definitive: "No more shall the sound of the millstone be heard in you, no more shall the light of a lamp shine in you, no more shall the voice of the bridegroom and the bride be heard in you" (Rev.18:22-23). The world of wickedness shall be brought to utter ruin.

But immediately, in contrast to this destruction of the world of wickedness, a loud song of praise rings forth in the heavens: "Alleluia. . . . Alleluia. . . . Alleluia! For the Lord our God the Almighty reigns. Let us rejoice and exult and give him the glory, for the marriage of the Lamb has come, and his Bride has made herself ready! . . . Blessed are those who are invited to the marriage supper of the Lamb!" (Rev.19:1,3,6-9).

The voice of the Bridegroom calls to his bride, his people, "Let me hear your voice, for your voice is sweet, and you are lovely" (Songs 2:14n). Her voice in response is the great hallel: "Alleluia! Proclaim the Lord for he is good, for his steadfast love endures forever!"

Hallel, "to celebrate," also meant "to give in marriage." To praise the Lord is to celebrate the marriage feast of the Lamb, in which he is united forever with his bride. The Eucharist on earth is our *todah,* our sacrifice of praise, foreshadowing the eternal wedding feast of heaven. Praise the Lord, for he is good, for his steadfast love endures forever!

Praise as Evangelization

The preceding chapters present much of the biblical background of what takes place at the prayer meeting held each Sunday by the Christian Community of God's Delight in Dallas, Texas. This meeting is evangelistic in nature. It is characterized by proclamation of the wonderful works of the Lord, as well as by the festal shout acclaiming his presence. God is glorified before all his people by the very acclamations which welcome him.

The festal shout, acclaiming the Lord present in our midst, amounts to saying, "He is risen! He is here! We are celebrating our own resurrection to life with him!" The acclamations are saying equivalently what Thomas said when he saw the risen Jesus: "My Lord and my God!" (John 20:28). This is the most basic act of Christian faith. It is a welcoming of Jesus, accepting him for what he truly is, Lord and God present with us always. It is the surrender of self to his lordship.

This acclamation is simultaneously a proclamation to everyone present that "Jesus is Lord" (1 Cor.12:3) and is here! For the manifest faith of those who are shouting to welcome Christ the King is itself a proclamation to others that he is truly risen and is with us. The very praise is announcing to everyone: "The Master is here, and is calling *you*" (John 11:28). That one sentence sums up the whole Gospel, the good news. The Gospel proclaims a reality here and now at work: the risen Lord is living in our midst, calling each one of us to himself, to give us eternal life. Newcomers to the prayer meeting, as they observe what is going on can only conclude, "Jesus really *is* Lord, and he *is* here, and he is calling *me*!"

When the initial praise subsides, and the assembled people settle quietly to listen to the Lord whom they have welcomed, all the words of prophecy and the inspired Scripture readings amount to saying the same thing: "The Master is here and is calling you!" Turn to him; you too welcome him; receive him into your lives; commit yourself to him.

Thus, the Sunday night prayer meeting is really evangelization, for it is a proclamation of the Lord and his saving presence. Present with us, he invites each one to turn more completely to him.

"Lord" is a dynamic title; it signifies action. It signifies Christ in action, exercising his dominion, using his saving power, filling with the power of the Holy Spirit all those who accept his presence. St. Paul gives a beautiful definition of Jesus Christ as Lord: "He is Son of God in power of sanctification through his resurrection from the dead" (Rom.4:4); he is "life-giving Spirit" (1 Cor.15:45), the one who gives the Holy Spirit, in whom we, too, come to life in Jesus.

My Christian act of faith, "My Lord and my God," means that I am yielding completely to him. I belong entirely to him in such a way that he works in me freely here and now.

From the midst of this joy in the Lord's presence come the individual testimonies to what this Lord has done and is doing in the personal lives of the people here present. This witness to the contemporary works of the Lord has meaning only in the context of the whole assembly. Just as the Israelite of old saw the personal favors of the Lord to him as a continuation of the blessings of the eternal covenant he had made with his whole people, so the contemporary charismatic Christian sees all the favors granted to him as a continuation of the wonderful work which is the Lord's resurrection. Just to acclaim him as *Lord* is to profess faith in his resurrection and in his abiding presence in which he continues to exercise his life-giving power. Every favor is granted to us in the risen Lord, and builds us up into the body of Christ, the Christian community. "For in him the whole fullness of deity dwells bodily, and you have come to fullness of life in him" (Col.2:9-10).

Though in faithfulness to his covenant, the Lord is present in their midst wherever two or three are gathered together in his name, that presence is most fully realized in the Eucharistic celebration. The same faith which is so vigorously proclaimed in the charismatic prayer meeting quietly and deeply acclaims his real presence in the Eucharistic sacrifice. The fact that our welcome to him in the Eucharistic celebration is not always that vociferous does not mean that he is any less present or any less active in the hearts of those who receive him in living faith. All the acclamations in the Eucharistic liturgy should be as heartfelt a welcome to him as any welcome extended to him in the enthusiams of a charismatic prayer meeting.

CHAPTER TEN

Praising God by Complaining

All that we have said so far has no doubt been misleading for those who praise God only when all is going well. For what we have said may have given the impression that we praise God only when he is near, only when we experience his presence.

But that is only half the picture. Biblical man praises God even when he seems to be very far away, even when it seems that he has abandoned us to our misery. The Book of Psalms has not only hymns of praise and joyous exaltation. It has also a large number of lamentations. "I pour out my complaint before him, I tell my trouble before him" (Ps.142:2). The lamentations are "complaints" addressed to God who seems to have forsaken the believer and to have withdrawn to a distance. And yet the believer continues to trust in God, and this trust is itself a form of praise.

A closer look at the psalms of lamentation shows that in reality they are a very true and eloquent form of praise. Perhaps the most sincere of all praise of God in this life is absolute faith and trust in him even when he seems to be an absent God, a silent God who does not seem to be near. The trust which the lamentations express is a tried and tested praise which rings true because it is being purified in trials. It testifies eloquently to the steadfast love and faithfulness of God whose ways are often disconcerting and beyond understanding. He seems to treat us badly, he seems unconcerned about our lot, and yet his love for us is ever steadfast.

The lamentations are themselves praise, because they honor the God of the covenant; they witness to his loving faithfulness to his covenant word, his word of promise. The complainer trusts in this covenant love even when all the evidence, his misery, seems to indicate that God no longer loves him, no longer is present with him.

The psalms of lamentation always contain three elements: a strong complaint to God because seemingly he is abandoning us to our troubles, a petition to save us from these troubles, and an act of wonderful trust and confidence in him because he is the God of covenant love and faithfulness.

But if the psalmist trusts so much in the God of the covenant, then why does he complain so much, why does he describe his misery in such detail? Because his trust in God does not minimize the reality of his misery. He really is suffering intensely, and he offers his troubles to the Lord in all their stark reality. His complaint is not a petulant blaming of God, but rather an unfolding of the facts of his troubles—laying them before the Lord, entrusting them to him. Though the description of his woes may sometimes give the impression that he is despairing, the mere fact that he shows them to the Lord and offers them to his love proves that he does trust. He is a man of faith, and this faith and trust is itself honor to God and praise of his goodness.

The psalmist does trust, and he is growing towards a deeper trust. "Lord, I do trust; help my lack of trust!" (cf., Mark 9:24). For even while he trusts the Lord, the flood of his troubles threatens to shake this trust, and so he cries out again to his God in a new act of confidence. And he praises the Lord, his Rock, his Strength. "I love you, O Lord, my strength. The Lord is my rock, and my fortress, and my deliverer, my God, my rock, in whom I take refuge, my shield, and the horn of my salvation, my stronghold. I call upon the Lord, who is worthy to be praised, and I am saved from my enemies" (Ps. 18:1-3). The Hebrew word for trust derives from the word for rock. The man who trusts in God is as firm and steadfast as God his Rock.

His complaining, moreover, is a reaching out for the freedom from all troubles which has been promised by the Lord in his covenant. Yet when this hope is deferred, the suffering one continues to trust, knowing that the Lord has his own excellent reasons for deferring the final fulfillment of his promises. In the very suffering, God is already working his salvation.

Psalm 74

The psalms of complaint, laying out all one's troubles before the Lord, are saying that even the fullness of trust in God does not cancel out the reality of suffering. It is precisely the intensity of the sufferings which requires trust in God, for he alone is man's hope. "I believed, even when I said, 'I am greatly afflicted'; I said in my alarm, 'No man is dependable.'" (Ps.116:10-11n). Before God, every man is "poor and needy."

Let us consider these ideas as expressed in Psalm 74. The whole psalm is a lament over the destruction of the temple, the place where God has always manifested his presence, the place where his Name dwelt. Though the destruction of the temple and the misery of the people would seem to indicate that God is gone and has forgotten his covenant, the psalmist in steadfast faith warns the people against disillusionment with their God and calls upon them to praise his name!

> Let not the downtrodden turn back in disillusion;
> let the poor and needy priase your name (Ps.74:21w).

These parallel lines are enlightening. In the parallelism of Hebrew poetry, a statement is made, and then the same thought is repeated in other words. In this case, we would expect the word "disillusion," or loss of trust, to be balanced by the words, "*trust* your name!" But instead, the psalmist uses "praise your name" as an equivalent for "trust your name." To praise God is to trust him, to trust him is to praise him. And to praise his name is to trust in his presence, though the temple, the place where his name dwelt, is destroyed.

The name, the presence, is still with them, and is contacted in sheer faith and trust, even when there is no external sign of his presence: "Deeds on our behalf we do not see; there is no prophet now" (Ps.74:9n).

The prophets had always been a sign of God's presence, for God spoke through them, recalling his people to covenant love. Even when the prophets spoke of doom, their words of warning and their call to conversion were at least a sign that God still cared enough for his people to chastize them, for their correction. But

when there is not even a prophet to threaten them—
"there is no prophet now" (Ps. 74:9)—surely God's love
must have reached the end of its patience! Does he no
longer care enough to correct his people? And yet the
psalmist says, "Let the poor and needy praise his name!"
Let them acclaim his presence though there seems to be
no signs that he is there! In calling the people to trust in
the God of the covenant, the psalmist is himself a true
prophet of the Lord, and he doesn't seem to know it!

Trust in God's Word

The presence of God is not always experienced in joy.
Sometimes it is accepted in the darkness of faith and the
dryness of hope and trust, even in the midst of trials and
sufferings. God is present and working for good even in
the most severe tribulations which man endures.

When everything is suffering or confusion, and there
seems to be no evidence at all of God's presence and
love, the believer learns to trust in God's word alone!

> When I am afraid, I put my trust in you,
> in God, whose *word* I praise,
> in God I trust without a fear.
> What can flesh do to me? (Ps.56:3-4).

Again in parallelism, we have "praise" and "trust" as
synonyms. Or rather, the synonyms are "trust in God"
and "praise of his word." The psalmist's fear is very real,
and in his lament he describes the strong reasons for his
fear. Yet when he fears, he trusts in the Lord's word.
This word is the Lord's word of promise, given in mak-

ing the covenant. In giving his word, the Lord has committed himself to those with whom he has made covenant.

Therefore because he trusts so absolutely in God, the psalmist relies completely on his word of promise, even though in his troubles he has no external evidence that God is keeping his word. But God's word is his only warrant of confidence: "I put my trust in you, in God whose *word* I praise." Another version translates it this way: "In you will I trust, in God in whose *promise* I glory" (Ps.56:4-5n). God's word is a promise which will infallibly be fulfilled. "Praise" or "glory" in this verse translates *hallel*, "to make clear, to celebrate." The psalmist glories in God's word of promise, he celebrates it, he rejoices in it even during his troubles, for God's word is absolutely trustworthy. Therefore in his troubles, the suffering man does not grudgingly praise God's word, he glories and exults in it! Such is his trust in the God of covenant love. This trust is truly beautiful praise of the ever faithful Lord. Truly, the psalms of trusting lamentation are always psalms of eloquent praise.

A Woman's Experience of Praise

At the time I was writing this chapter, a Dallas woman, the mother of three small children, who had experienced serious trials in her life in the past few months, came to me and told me what praise of God had done in her life. She said:

> When I first came to know the Lord, I would praise God joyfully whenever things were going well

for me. But as soon as things seemed to go wrong, I would get angry with God, and resent his ways in my life. But now at last, and only recently, I have learned how to praise him even in the midst of my troubles. I no longer resent anything that happens in my life, but praise God for everything.

Then she opened her bible to Ephesians and pointed to a verse which she had not only underlined, but around which she had drawn a box so that the words seemed to stand out from the rest of the page:

Sing the words and tunes of the psalms and hymns when you are together, and GO ON SINGING AND CHANTING TO THE LORD IN YOUR HEARTS, so that always and everywhere you are giving thanks to God who is our Father in the name of our Lord Jesus Christ (Eph.5:19-20*j*).

She said that the boxed words (the ones we have printed in capitals) express perfectly how she now experiences the praise of God. The praise is a pure gift from God poured out into her heart; it is not something that she does; it is something that God does in her. It is a powerful presence of God in her heart. In this praise she is enjoying his presence, and the experience is so overwhelming that at times she has to stop everything she is doing. For example, one day as she was driving on the expressway, the presence of God with her in the midst of this praise he was fashioning in her was so overwhelming that she would have stopped the car had that been safe in the heavy rush of traffic.

Reflecting on this woman's testimony, we notice three

stages in the evolution of the grace of praise in her life. At first, when she sang songs and hymns together with the charismatic community, she praised God in the joy of being with him in the company of the community. But when she went home and her troubles overwhelmed her, she resented the Lord because he was allowing these things to happen to her, and was not working a miracle to remove them. But in time, and through effort, she learned to praise God even in her hardships, which were truly great. It was this which opened her up to the third stage, in which God himself poured out into her heart a grace of praise which was simultaneously an experience of his presence.

No doubt there will be further stages. There will be times of darkness, when she will have to continue to trust. She will have to praise not only in consolation, but also in desolation and abandonment by the Lord.

Another's Struggle to Praise

Four days later, another woman told me that she had been very angry with God when the large airliner crashed in Vietnam with hundreds of refugee children abroad. And when someone reminded her of the words of Yahweh in Isaiah, "My ways are not your ways" (Isa.55:8), she said that these words were only an excuse God gives to explain away his failure to act to relieve our misery.

But then she happened to read Psalm 143, and suddenly her frustration was turned into trust. She realized the sinfulness of her resentment of God and came to confess her sin. "God is trying to tell me something in all this," she said. So I said to her, "Yes, this is what the

Lord is saying to you: 'Your anger against me is itself a kind of praise of me, because at least it amounts to saying: I expect the Lord to act and take care of my troubles; I admit that he can do it, and this itself is witness that he is God. But the very fact that you complain when I do not act to extricate you in your way is witness to your narrowness and your own helplessness. So admit your neediness, and trust me! Trust my ways, not yours. I know what I am about.' "

From Complaining Praise to Wordless Joy.

A little later, still another woman came to me to tell me how praise had grown in her heart. She had been sick for many years, but had been healed by God when she trusted him and expressed this trust in praise. She said:

When I was helpless, flat on my back, I praised the Lord verbally, with faith in the future; I praised him for what I hoped he would do for me in the future; I praised him for the physical cure I hoped he would grant me.

But while I was still helpless, gradually I learned to praise him for the situation here and now, for my sickness and helplessness, knowing in faith and trust that everything is all right even here and now, because Jesus is Lord, and works in all things for the good of those who love him.

After that, I began to discover that I am now always praising God in my heart in a wordless way, in great freedom, the freedom of love and joy.

91

About six months later the same woman came to see me again, and spoke of a further evolution in her ways of praising God:

> *I began by praising God for the good things he does for me personally, the many little favors he grants me in his love.*
>
> *Then I reached a point when the emphasis in my praise was not on the things he does for me, but on who he is, and what he is.*
>
> *Then my praise went even beyond that, and I began to praise him for the magnificent way he works in everything, in an astonishing way that surpasses all our expectations and understanding: "My ways are not your ways." He is Lord of everything, and his glory is clear in everything he does, for he is giving of himself in everything. Everything he does reveals who he is.*

The woman was trying to express her awareness that all the works of the Lord are works of self-giving. No longer could she be content just to thank and praise him for the little things he did in her life. She now saw an all-pervading presence and purpose of God in the whole universe, working wonders exceedingly surpassing all our expectations. The God who is so marvelous in himself is revealing himself and pouring himself out, as it were, in all his marvelous workings in everything, especially in all that he does in our lives, so that his own joy may be in us. "Bless the Lord, all you works of the Lord, praise and exalt him above all forever" (Dan.3:57n).

CHAPTER ELEVEN

Psalm 22

In some of the psalms of lamentation, the lamenting one bolsters his wavering trust by promising to bring a sacrifice of praise to God when he has been delivered. He reminds himself that the faithful God will somehow turn his sorrow into joy, and this joy will be expressed in loving praise (e.g., Ps.69:30-36). In other lamentations, the poet's confidence in the Lord is so firm that already in advance he expresses explicit praise and thanksgiving for the expected deliverance (e.g., Ps.56,62).

Psalm 22—"My God, my God, why have you forsaken me?"—is an outstanding example of a lamentation which bursts into joyous praise. No doubt it was composed for a *todah*, a sacrifice of praise. The psalmist first dramatizes the depths of his misery, the misery from which the Lord rescues him. Then he sings his song of thanksgiving and praise for the deliverance.

It is important to note to whom the psalmist addresses his complaint in the first part of this psalm. He says, "My God, my God." "My God" is a covenant name. It echoes the great covenant formula used by the Lord, "I will be their God and they shall be my people"

93

(Jer.31:33). The very fact that the lament is addressed to the God of the covenant implies faith that the Lord will be faithful to his covenant, and can be trusted to act on behalf of the suffering one. To call upon him as "my God" is already an act of trust, no matter how desperate the complaint seems to be, no matter how deep the anguish and seeming despair from which it springs.

God seems to be very far removed from the psalmist both in space—"Why are you far from my weeping, from the words of my crying?"—and in time—"I call by day, and you answer me not, by night, and I find no rest." But even so he trusts, and expreses the reason for his trust: his God is the God of the covenant, who has always been close to his people and is their King, acclaimed with praise: "You are holy, enthroned on the praises of Israel." You are there with your people, who welcome you in praise.

That he is addressing the God of the covenant is confirmed by the reasons he gives for his trust: "Our fathers" (the people of the covenant who were our ancestors) "trusted in you, and you delivered them . . . in you they trusted, and were not disappointed." You were faithful to your covenant with them, you will be faithful to your covenant with me, for it is one and the same covenant into which you entered with them and with me. Your faithful love for them is the pledge of your faithful love for me.

The psalmist returns to his lament, for the expected deliverance is still far away. He tells how everyone has turned against him (v. 7), and God is his only hope. Everyone jeers at him, mocking even his trust in God: "He committed his cause to the Lord; let him deliver him, let him resuce him, for he delights in him" (v. 8).

His enemies hint that his trust in God has been in vain, for God is still absent from him.

These jeers do not shake his trust, but only cause him to reaffirm it: I was born into covenant faith and trust, "from my mother's womb you are *my God*." You cared for me then—"you are he who took me from the womb"—you will care for me now. "Be not far from me, for trouble is near me, and there is no one to rescue me." You are my only hope!

The complaint continues, as he describes the intensity of his enemies' attacks upon him. They are like bulls and lions, the strongest of the beasts, they are like bandits and bloodhounds. His strength drains away like water, his thirst burns like fire. He is at the extreme of all misery: they have stripped him of his garments, and he is naked and defenseless, readied for execution (v. 12-18). And yet he continues to trust, and repeats his prayer for help, enumerating the many evils from which the Lord will save him (v.19-21).

This psalm, very artfully composed, expresses a profound truth of Israel's covenant experience: no matter what the miseries one is enduring, one can offer them to God in confident trust, and in God's good time, such a one will praise God in joy because he has delivered him. In the lamentation part of the psalm (v. 1-22), the poet piles suffering upon suffering, and thus dramatizes his personal troubles as a symbol of all the worst that any man has to suffer. In the praise part (v. 23-32), he celebrates his personal deliverance as a pledge and symbol of the universal deliverance promised to all mankind. Just as in the lament he dramatized every evil that man can endure, so in the praise he pictures every imaginable blessing that God can bestow, every possible benefit that man can hope for. From all evils God will rescue his people, pouring out all the positive blessings which will replace these evils.

Thus, in contrast to the enmity and attacks from his fellowmen, he describes the marvelous unity of mankind in which all will be united in praising God. His own deliverance from the deepest depths of his misery inspires him to call upon every category of human being to join him in praising the Lord. First, he calls upon his brothers, the people of Israel, to praise the Lord, because he has rescued him from all his afflictions (v. 22-26). But this praise, in the midst of the assembly (v. 25), will in turn inspire all the nations to come to the Lord in worship (v. 27-28). All categories of men shall join in this praise: not only those now living, but also those who have gone down into the dust in death (v. 29), and all generations yet to be born, for his posterity will carry on the praise from age to age (v. 30-31).

The poet himself has been rescued from death; hence his conviction that "all who go down to the dust" will live to praise the Lord. And because God brought him forth from the womb in the first place that he might live, so he calls upon all who shall be brought from the womb in the ages to come, "a people yet to be born," to join him in praising the Lord. In his troubles he has experienced a solidarity with all suffering mankind, so now he calls upon them all for solidarity with him in hope and in trust and in universal praise of the Lord.

All those who join him in the *todah*, the sacrificial meal of praise and thanksgiving, are, like himself, "afflicted" and "poor" (v. 26). But they shall eat this meal with praise, even though they are still seeking the Lord from the midst of their trials and neediness: "The afflicted shall eat and be satisfied, those who seek him shall praise the Lord" (v. 26). Even while they are still seeking, already they praise him, so firm is their trust in him. Their trust is based on the experience of their fathers in the covenant, who trusted before them (v. 5).

The poet's great intuition, then, is this: no matter what your troubles, trust in God, and you will praise him in joy when he rescues you. He tries to portray the extremity of distress, saying that even then you can trust.

Jesus trusted in his Father in this way when he prayed this psalm from the depths of his horrible misery as he hung on the cross. Everything seemed to indicate that the Father had totally abandoned him. But the very fact that he cried out to the God of the covenant in the words of this lamentation, "My God, my God, why have you forsaken me," indicates that his trust was unshaken. In praying a lamentation psalm, one confidently entrusts his miseries to God. If Jesus had abandoned hope, he would no longer have addressed a prayer to his Father. But he did not despair, he did not fail to trust, and thus praise his Father. The completeness of his confidence is expressed in the other psalm which he prayed as he died, "Father, into your hands I commit my spirit" (Luke 23:46). Those words, too, spring from the midst of a psalm of lamentation (Ps.31:5). The whole of Psalm 31, like Psalm 22, illustrates beautifully how lamentation and praise are but two sides of one coin, and how trust is itself perfect praise.

Jesus is the great Amen to the intuition of Psalm 22. In him, not only are all sufferings piled upon sufferings, but in him too all blessings are piled upon blessings, blessings for all the nations, past, present and to come, the dead of the past, the living of the present, the unborn of the future. His deliverance from death in his resurrection is not only a sign and pledge of all this, but in his risen person the full reality is already present, to be communicated in turn to those who trust in him.

This psalm on the lips of Jesus dying on the cross explains the profound meaning of his death and resurrection. His trust in God has been rewarded with the sum total of the blessings that man can hope for. All the afflicted who trust in the Lord are invited to celebrate the Christian *todah*, the Eucharist, the sacrificial meal of praise which is the pledge of the full celebration of the Lamb's eternal wedding feast with his bride, the Church. Verse 27 finds its fullest meaning in the Eucharist: "The lowly shall eat their fill; they who seek the Lord shall praise him: 'May your hearts be ever merry!' " (Ps.22: 27n). They praise the Lord by sharing their joy with their fellowmen.

Created to Praise

"Will the dust praise you, will it tell of your faithfulness?" asks another psalmist's lament (Ps.30:19). The answer is given unequivocally in the risen Jesus. Yes indeed the dust will praise the Lord: "Before him alone must all who sleep in the earth prostrate themselves, before him must all bow who go down into the dust!" (Ps.22:30). "At the name of Jesus every knee should bow, in heaven and on earth and under the earth, and every tongue confess that Jesus Christ is Lord!" (Phil. 2:10). Because he became obedient unto death, God exalted him as Lord and gave him power to give life to all the dead.

When Jesus said, on the cross, "My God, my God, why have you forsaken me," he was addressing the faithful God of the covenant, expressing his personal trust in him. That his God has been faithful to the covenant is manifest in the resurrection of Jesus, and is expressed by Jesus in his words after his resurrection, "I am ascending to my Father and your Father, to my God and your God" (John 20:17). These words echo the traditional covenant formula, "I will be their God and they shall be my people." God has fulfilled his covenant with Israel in the new and eternal covenant in the blood of his Son. "All the promises of God find their Yes in Jesus. That is why we utter the Amen through him, to the glory of God" (2 Cor.1:20).

CHAPTER TWELVE

Repentance as Praise

In the Latin Bible used by St. Augustine, the words of the *todah* psalms, "Proclaim the Lord, for he is good, for his steadfast love endures forever," were, "Confitemini Domino quoniam bonus, quoniam in saeculum misericordia ejus." *Confitemini* means to confess, to glorify, to praise. "Confess to the Lord, for he is good, for his mercy endures forever."

That is exactly what Augustine does in his famous *Confessions*. The *Confessions* are praise of God. Only secondarily are they the confession of Augustine's sinful life; primarily they are the confession of God's goodness and mercy. Augustine confesses his sins only in order to confess the mercy of God who has rescued him from these sins and has brought him into the direct experience of God in love. The whole book is addressed to God as praise: "I confess unto men in your sight by this book not what I once was, but what I now am."[31]

In this book, Augustine has a great deal to say about praising God. On the opening page he tells us that man was created to praise God and to find his joy and peace in this praise. He begins by confessing to God in the presence of men:

> Great are you, O Lord, and greatly to be praised (Ps.145:3). Great is your power, and of your wisdom there is no number (Ps.147:5). And man desires to praise you. . . . This tiny part of all that you have created desires to praise you. You so arouse him that to praise you is his joy. For you have made us for yourself, O Lord, and our hearts are restless till they rest in you.[32]

Augustine gives his reasons for confessing publicly the specific wonderful things that God has done for him personally. These are basically the same reasons given in the psalms for the *todah*, the sacrifice of praise. Psalm 40, composed for a *todah*, declares, "He drew me up from the desolate pit. . . and set my feet upon a rock. . . . He put a new song in my mouth, a song of praise to our God. Many will see and fear, *and put their trust in the Lord*" (Ps.40:2-3).

Augustine elaborates beautifully upon this reason. By confessing how God has mercifully rescued him from sin, he arouses hope and trust in the hearts of the discouraged and despairing:

> When the confessions of my past sins—which you have forgiven and covered up, giving me joy in you, changing my life by faith and your sacrament—are read and heard, they stir up the heart. The heart no longer lies in the lethargy of despair and says "I cannot," but keeps wakeful in the love of your mercy and the loveliness of your grace, by which every weak man is made strong, since by it he is made conscious of his weakness.

As for good people, it rejoices them to hear of sins committed in the past by men now free from them: not because these things are sins, but because they were and no longer are. . . . I confess not what I once was, but what I am now![33]

But will people believe Augustine's confessions, will they respond to them in the way he hopes, or will they "turn him off" in incredulity and ridicule? Augustine runs this risk, and makes his confessions before men of good will: love believes what is spoken in love! "Because charity believes all things, that is, all things spoken by those whom it binds to itself and makes one, I, O Lord, confess to you that men may hear, for though I cannot prove to them that my confession is true, yet those will believe me whose ears charity has opened to me."[34]

Augustine realizes that God's saving work in him is not yet finished. Conversion is an on-going process, it is a spiritual combat. Therefore he confesses not only to glorify God for what he has done in saving him, but also to obtain the help of intercessory prayers asking that God will bring to perfection what he has begun: "They rejoice with me when they hear how close by your grace I have come to you, Lord, and pray for me when they hear how far I am held from you by my own weight. To such shall I show myself."[35]

At contemporary charismatic prayer meetings, those who confess to God's mercy, praising him for rescuing them from sin, are not always as aware as Augustine was that they should also ask the prayers of the community for their perseverence in the way of salvation, even while they praise and thank God for saving them. They should realize that in a very true sense they are only beginning their walk on the road of conversion and salvation. Like Augustine they should say:

> It is no small fruit (of my confessions), O Lord my God, that many should give thanks to you for me, and many should pray to you for me. . . . (Let my brethren) rejoice for what they see good in me, and grieve for what they see ill, but whether they see good or ill still love me. To such shall I show myself.[36]

Augustine confesses before the whole communion of saints, those of past, present, and future: "I confess in the ears of the believing sons of men, companions of my joy and sharers of my mortality, my fellow citizens, fellow pilgrims: those who have gone before, and those who are to come after, and those who walk in the way of life with me."[37]

Once again we see Augustine's consciousness of his solidarity with all God's redeemed people, not only of the present, but also those of the past and of the future. In this he is true to the Scriptures. He is like the psalmist who calls upon all mankind to praise the Lord who has rescued him: not only his living brothers in Israel (Ps.22:22-25), but all the nations of mankind (v. 27-28), and all those who have already gone down into the dust of death (v.29), and all those who are yet to be born (v.30-31). All these shall live with him to praise the Lord (v.26). "For I think upon the price of my redemption, I eat it and drink it and give it to others to eat and drink; and being poor I desire to be filled with it among the poor: 'The poor shall eat and be satisfied; those who seek him shall praise the Lord!' (Ps.22:26)."[38] Here, of course, Augustine is referring to the Eucharist, in which we celebrate our salvation in solidarity with the saved of all mankind. Like the psalmists, Augustine sees the personal benefits God has bestowed on him as a sharing in and continuation of the salvation he has granted to his whole people in the blood of his Son. All rejoice together, all help one another to share fully in this salvation.

Augustine knows that he is still weak and prone to sin. All that is his own is his sinfulness, all that is good in him is from God. These are further reasons for confessing. "When I am wicked, confession to you, O Lord, simply means being displeased with myself; when I am good, confession to you means not attributing my goodness to myself."[39] Bearing witness to God's favors is not boasting. It is glorifying God and giving him the credit.

The Penitential Rite as Praise

In the New Testament, the term "sacrifice of praise" occurs in Hebrews: "Through (Jesus) then let us continually offer up a sacrifice of praise to God, that is, the fruit of lips that acknowledge his name" (Heb.13:15). The "fruit of lips" means the words in which we confess what the Lord has done for us; and this we do especially in the Eucharistic celebration. We proclaim that we are sinners whom the Lord has saved by his death and resurrection, and who eat and drink the price of our redemption.

The term "fruit of lips" is taken from Hosea 14:2 and Isaiah 57:18. In Hosea, it means words of sincere repentance: "Take with you words, and return to the Lord; say to him, 'Take away all iniquity, accept that which is good, and we will render the fruit of our lips' " (Hos. 14:2). That is, if you grant us forgiveness, our hearts and our lips will offer our praise. "The fruit of lips" is praise and thanksgiving for the reconciliation granted by God.

Another version of Hosea translates the verse thus: "Instead of bulls, we will *consecrate our lips* to you" (Hos.14:2b). Our lips and our lives will be lovingly dedicated to joyous praise of God who is love. This praise will be the spontaneous overflowing of joy in God's merciful goodness. "I will praise the name of God in song, and I will glorify him with thanksgiving; this will please the Lord more than oxen or bullocks with horns and divided hooves" (Ps.69:31-32n). God is pleased with praise because he is pleased with the reconciliation and the joyous love of which it is the overflowing.

According to Isaiah, God himself creates this praise on our lips by granting healing and comfort through his word of peace and reconciliation: " 'But I will heal him, and console him, I will comfort him to the full, both him and his afflicted fellows, bringing praise to their lips (creating the fruit of lips—r). Peace, peace to far and near, I will indeed heal him,' says Yahweh" (Isa.57: 18-19j).

St. Paul applies these words of Isaiah to Jesus and to the proclamation of the Gospel: "He came and 'announced the good news of peace to you who were far off, and to those who were near' " (Eph.2:17n). The Eucharistic Prayer, "the sacrifice of praise, that is, the fruit of lips," is a proclamation of this good news of peace and reconciliation granted to us in the sacrifice of Jesus. The desolation and sorrow caused by sin has been taken away by "the voice of the Bridegroom," the Lamb of God:

In this place of which you say, "It is a waste without man or beast"... there shall be heard again the voice of mirth and the voice of gladness, the voice of the bridegroom and the voice of the bride, the voices of those who sing as they bring thank offerings (the sacrifice of praise) to the house of the Lord: "Give thanks (praise) to the Lord of hosts, for the Lord is good, for his steadfast love endures forever!" (Jer.33:10-11)

The Eucharistic proclamation is a call to accept the reconciliation brought by the Lamb and to rejoice in his love. The old Dominican Rite caught this Eucharistic spirit of proclamation and praise in a beautiful way, and, in the words of Jeremiah (33:10), began the Eucharistic celebration with the immediate proclamation of that joy: "*Confitemini Domino quoniam bonus*: Praise the Lord for he is good, for his mercy endures forever." The people responded at once by accepting the joy of reconciliation with God through confession of their sins in repentance: "*Confiteor Deo*: I confess to Almighty God. . ." In the Latin, there is a manifest correspondence between the opening word of the proclamation, *Confitemini*, and the opening word of the penitential response, *Confiteor*. Because I can confess God's mercy and steadfast love, I can confess my sins with courage, knowing I will be forgiven and reconciled with the Father in the blood of the Lamb. *Confitemini—Confiteor*: to confess our sins to him is to praise the Lord, for it is to glorify him for his merciful forgiveness.

Though this beautiful penitential rite was abandoned by the Dominicans after Vatican II, it may still be used by anyone celebrating the new Roman liturgy. For the thought, "Let us prepare ourselves to celebrate this sacred liturgy by calling to mind our sins," is more richly expressed by saying, "Confess the Lord, for he is good, for his mercy endures forever," thus inviting the humble confession, "I confess to Almighty God, etc." Such an opening proclamation at the beginning of the Eucharistic liturgy is already saying implicitly, "The Lamb of God, who takes away the sin of the world, is here! Acclaim him, confess your sins to him, and your joy will overflow in praise, 'the fruit of lips which acknowledge his name' " (Heb.13:15).

CHAPTER THIRTEEN

Bless the Lord, O My Soul!

> The Lord said to Moses: "Speak to Aaron and his
> sons and tell them: This is how you shall bless the
> Israelites. Say to them:
>   The Lord bless you and keep you!
>   The Lord les his face shine upon you, and be
> gracious to you!
>   The Lord look upon you kindly and give you
> peace!
> So shall they invoke my name upon the Israelites,
> and I will bless them. (Num.6:22-27n)

The abundant flow of God's blessings in response to
this invocation in faith evoked in turn from the heart of
men grateful acknowledgement of these blessings and of
the God who blesses. Blessing is mutual communion
between God and his worshippers. The verb "to bless"
(*barak*) signifies both the descending movement of God's
favor and grace, and the ascending movement of human
recognition and acknowledgement. It is a virtuous circle.
When man blesses God, acknowledging the Lord's favors

of the past in praise and thanksgiving, God blesses man, granting new favors in the present.

This ascending and descending movement of blessing was an integral element in the temple liturgy of Israel, where, in faithfulness to his covenant with his people, God continued to manifest his favors to them: "Come bless the Lord, all you servants of the Lord. . . . Lift up your hands to the holy place, and bless the Lord! May the Lord bless you from Zion, he who made heaven and earth!" (Ps.134).

Thus, when Israel blessed the Lord for the divine favors of the past, it was in full expectation that the Lord's faithfulness would continue these favors in the present. For all favors granted by the Lord at any time—past, present or future—were considered as granted in his perennial faithfulness to his covenant.

Sometimes a blessing is addressed to God as sheer praise and thanksgiving. At other times it is inseparable from the invocation of God's blessing upon a fellowman: "Blessed be Abram by God Most High, the creator of heaven and earth; and blessed be God Most High, who delivered your foes into your hand" (Gen.14:19-20n). This is a typical formula of blessing, expressing both the descending and ascending movement of blessing.

So certain was Israel of God's covenant love that her people had no hesitation whatever in pronouncing God's blessing over one another. Just to say the word of blessing was enough to bring God's blessing upon the person over whom this word was pronounced. For the word of blessing, enunciated with faith in God's covenant love, was a word of power, effectively calling upon the Lord's faithfulness to his promises.

Therefore in invoking a blessing upon one's fellowman, one usually began by blessing God, praising him for the blessings of the past, which are a pledge of continuing blessings in the present and future; but above all praising him as Lord and Creator, and God of the covenant with Israel. To bless God is to attribute everything to him, acknowledging him as the source of all blessings:

> Blessed may you be, O Lord, God of Israel our father, from eternity to eternity. Yours, O Lord, are grandeur and power, majesty, splendor, and glory. For all in heaven and on earth is yours. Yours, O Lord, is the sovereignty; you are exalted as head over all. Riches and honor are from you, and you have dominion over all. In your hand are power and might. It is yours to give grandeur and strength to all.
>
> Therefore our God we give you thanks, and we praise the majesty of your name. (1 Chron.29:10-13n)

A blessing invoked upon one's fellowman, then, is firmly rooted in praise of God, with complete confidence that he will continue to bless. Such confidence is not presumptuous. It is simply claiming what God has promised in his covenant commitment to care for his people and provide for their needs. God is forever present among his people in faithfulness to his promises. The liturgy of praise and blessing is an acclaiming of this presence. It is an opening of self to this presence and to the favors it brings.

Thus, to bless the Lord was not simply to acknowledge his gifts. It was above all a grateful recognition of the Giver. To bless the Lord is to acclaim him as the loving source of all blessings, and to rejoice in him because he is what he is, the God of all goodness.

God's supreme blessing to men is the gift of himself to them, that they might live in communion with him. This indeed is the eternal gift, the irrevocable gift, of which other blessings are but tokens and pledges. Other blessings may be ephemeral, his gift of himself remains forever.

St. Augustine expresses this beautifully in his commentary on the words of the psalm, "I will bless the Lord at all times, his praise shall continually be in my mouth" (Ps.34:1). Speaking first of God's lesser gifts, Augustine says, "You must bless him when he bestows these gifts, and bless him when he takes them away. For it is he who gives and he who takes away (Job 1:21), but himself he never takes away from one who blesses him" (On Ps.37).[40] To bless him is to possess him, for to bless him is to acknowledge and accept his abiding presence as source of all blessings.

Therefore we continue to praise God even if he seems to take all his other blessings away from us, for himself he never takes away. That is why charismatics insist upon praising God even in the midst of the most difficult tribulations and trials, acclaiming the Lord who is still with them even though he may seem to be absent. "The Lord gave, and the Lord has taken away; blessed be the name of the Lord!" (Job 1:21).

"You Will Be A Blessing"

One afternoon I received a phone call from a doctor

111

of psychiatry, a member of the Christian Community of God's Delight. At a community meeting, I had asked the members for testimony about what praise means in their lives, and he was calling in response to this request. As the doctor spoke, I realized that his experience of praise resembles in many ways the experience of St. Augustine. Augustine, we have seen, experienced jubilation as joy that God is what he is. But he experienced this in consciousness of the whole body of Christ. Both for Augustine and for the doctor, joyous praise is a distinct awareness of the presence of God and is a community experience. I present the doctor's own words as I took them down as he spoke:

> There was a time when I thought that praise was not the primary thing in the charismatic renewal. But now I know that it is as fundamental as anything. In praise, I experience a kind of new relationship with God which I had not thought of before— relating to him simply because he is God!
>
> Five years ago, in a retreat under Ralph Martin, I had my first experience of free and open vocal expression of praise with a community, including dancing and singing. I received the baptism of the Spirit under these circumstances, in completely free praise and singing. My baptism in the Spirit was preceded and followed by singing and praise. Shortly afterwards I had the experience of the Holy Spirit as a definite and distinct personality.
>
> My awareness of coming into the presence of God is definitely related to open and vocal praise. When I pray, the first thing I do is praise, to bring myself into his presence. It used to be that I felt

God's presence and could come into his presence only early in the morning in the church, in the presence of the Blessed Sacrament. That was my most significant help in bringing myself into his presence. But now, praising, even more than the quiet of the sanctuary, brings me into God's presence.

My praising of God is also now so much more a relationship with other people. I feel the community in praise even when I am not with them. Thus there are two elements in my praise: it brings me into the presence of God, and gives me the experience of community. In praising God I am always aware of all the brothers and sisters in the Lord.

I crave a more spontaneous praise at Mass. In my awareness of the others present at the Mass, I want to praise!

In praise, I experience a deeper relationship with my family, with my parish, and with the other parishes and places where I have worshipped in the past.

For me the charismatic relationship has been one of brother and sister. The family of God is so different for me now. I am aware of it all day long. Awareness of God's presence is so much a part of every moment of my day. When I awake at night, I think of God. I think of him first. There is a greater tendency than formerly to verbalize even then, to verbalize praise without being loud enough to be heard or to disturb others.

When I pray at home, I bless not only my family, but I bless the whole neighborhood and the parish.

In connection with blessing the neighborhood: last week a boy bicycling to my home ran into an automobile and his head went through the windshield. Though one-hundred and seventy-six stitches had to be made in his head, he was not even knocked unconscious, not a muscle was wrenched; and the next day, after the initial shock had passed, he was feeling fine. Blessing the neighborhood in our praise of God is extremely important.

When I go into a restaurant to eat, I bless everyone in the restaurant, calling down God's blessings on them. Extending our blessings to others in our personal prayer is something new for me, but extremely important. Singing "Bless the Lord, O my soul!" excites me.

Be a Blessing!

I can understand why the doctor finds the song, "Bless the Lord, O my soul," so moving. We said that in the Scriptures a *berakah*, an invocation of a blessing, always begins with praise of God, the source of all blessings. The people who bless the Lord become a blessing for all those among whom they live. This was the mission given to Abraham and to his descendants. "The men of faith . . . are the sons of Abraham" (Gal. 3:7). To Abraham God said, "I will make your name great, so that *you will be a blessing*. . . . All the communities of the earth shall find blessing in you" (Gen.12: 2-3n). And again he said to him, "In your descendants all the nations of the earth shall find blessing" (Gen 22:18).

114

God's people, then, are to be a blessing for others. Elsewhere, God's people are described as "the people who bless the Lord" (Judg.5:2n), "a people whom I formed for myself, that they might announce my praise" (Isa.43:21n).

In experiencing the whole community whenever he praises God, and in feeling the need to call down God's blessing upon them all when he praises, the doctor is experiencing in a living way an essential aspect of God's people: they are a blessing for other people. In the original French of the Jerusalem Bible, God's words to Abraham are translated in the imperative: "Be a blessing!" (Gen.12:2b).

PART THREE

The Eucharist:
"The Sacrifice of Praise"

CHAPTER FOURTEEN

"Father, Glorify Your Name!"

In his great prayer of praise at the Last Supper, "Father....glorify your Son, so that the Son may glorify you" (John 17:1*j*), Jesus tells the Father that *his whole life* on earth has been a sacrifice of praise: "I have glorified you on earth!" (John 17:4*j*).

Jesus did indeed frequently glorify the Father *in words* during his time on earth. He prayed the psalms of praise as one with the Jewish people into which he had been born. When he sang, "Bless the Lord, O my soul! ... As a father pities his children, so the Lord pities those who fear him" (Ps.103:1,13), he must have thrilled with love for his heavenly Father. St. Luke tells us explicitly how one day Jesus "thrilled with joy in the Holy Spirit and said, 'I bless you, Father...'" (Luke 10:21*b*).

He taught his disciples to begin all their prayer with a desire that the Father be praised: "Say, 'Father... hallowed by your name'" (Luke 11:2). He practised what he preached when, faced with death, he praised the Father, saying, "Father, glorify your name!" (John 12:28).

119

But when he says at the Last Supper, "Father, I glorified you on earth," he is not referring to the glory he has given to God in words; he is speaking of his whole life and of his deeds in fulfilling his mission from the Father: "I glorified you on earth, having accomplished the work which you gave me to do" (John 17:4). His whole life in fulfillment of his mission has thus been praise of God. He has glorified the Father by living completely for him.

Especially, Jesus sees his death as praise of the Father. As he speaks on the first Palm Sunday about his coming death, referring to himself as a grain of wheat falling into the ground and dying, he is suddenly overwhelmed with fear. His first impulse is to ask to be freed from the necessity of dying: "Now is my soul troubled. And what shall I say? 'Father, save me from this hour'? No! For this purpose I have come to this hour. Father, glorify thy name!" (John 12:27-28). He accepts death, for the Father's glory!

A few verses later, Jesus refers to his coming crucifixion. "I, when I am lifted up from the earth, will draw all men to myself." John adds, "He said this to show by what death he was to die" (John 12:32-33).

The Lord's death is his supreme praise of the Father, for by giving his very life, he ratifies all the words of praise he has ever uttered, and puts his seal upon their sincerity.

Indeed, his death is the continuation and completion of the praise which he had expressed so eloquently when he thrilled with joy in the Holy spirit and praised the Father (Luke 10:21). For in his death he remained true to the divine sonship in which he had rejoiced on that occasion. For his joy in revealing the Father to the little ones was but an overflowing of his joy in loving his Father as a beloved son. The same love for the Father perdures throughout his passion and death. His faithfulness to the Father even unto death is rooted in the profound joy in the Father which he had experienced during his earthly life.

For that thrill of joy in the Holy Spirit which burst forth as praise from his lips could only have welled up from the deep abiding joy in his Father which was ever in his heart. He had always deeply experienced the Father's love for Him. "You are my beloved Son; with you I am well pleased" (Mark 1:11). "As the Father has loved me, so have I loved you" (John 15:9).

Even when this thrill of joy was gone as he hung on the cross and cried out his lamentation, "My God, my God, why have you forsaken me," Jesus continued to act out of consciousness of the Father and love for him. He acted like the Son he was; he continued to respond to the love he had always experienced, the love to which he had responded in that thrill of joy in the Holy Spirit.

That love of the Father for him now seems to be hidden as he hangs on the cross, yet Jesus continues to trust in it. He expresses this filial trust in his prayer of lamentation, "My God, my God, why have you forsaken me?" In the succeeding words of that psalm, he continues to claim God as his Father, though his enemies taunt him for this. "You are he who took me from the womb. . . . Upon you was I cast from my birth, and since my mother bore me you have been my God" (Ps. 22:9-10). I will not now renounce the one who has always been my Father, though my enemies cry out to me, "Come down off that cross if you are God's son!" (Matt.27:40n).

121

At the Last Supper when he offered himself in sacrifice, he promised his disciples a share in his own joy in the Father: "As the Father has loved me, so have I loved you; abide in my love. . . . These things I have spoken to you that my joy may be in you, and that your joy may be full" (John 15:9-11) He is speaking of his joy as Son of God, the joy he has in God his Father. And he prays that the Father will grant this joy to us: "that they may have my joy fulfilled in themselves" (John 17:13).

The joy he has in his Father's love for him is transmitted to his disciples in the Father's love which he bestows upon them: "Father, you have loved them even as you have loved me" (John 17:23). Jesus is fully aware of his power to give us the Father's love, and in that love to give us the Father's life and joy: "You have given the Son power over all flesh, to give eternal life to all whom you have given him" (John 17:2).

Thus, our Lord praises the Father at the Last Supper, and on the cross, for the same reasons that he praised him when he thrilled with joy in the Holy Spirit because the Father was revealing himself through him. Through his death, his Father's love will be revealed, his Father's life will be given to men. In his Last Supper prayer, he expresses his desire that the Father be praised and glorified as the fruit of his work of revealing him: "I have glorified you on earth, I have accomplished the work you have given me to do. . . . I have manifested your name to the men you gave me out of the world" (John 17:4-6).

These are the reasons for the Lord's own jubilation as it is continued in the hearts of Christians. We thrill with joy in the Holy Spirit and cry out our supreme word of praise, "Abba, Father! Hallowed be your name!" But God is best praised when he is accepted as Father through our living as his true sons. "Father, I have glorified you on earth. I have accomplished the work you have given me to do" (John 17:4).

Praise and Suffering

Christian praise and joy is always rooted in the paschal mystery of Jesus: his death and resurrection. It springs forth most radiantly and ardently from those who have experienced redemption in Jesus from sin or suffering.

Suffering and death, Jesus tells us, prepare a greater glory for God. When Mary and Martha wonder why Jesus did not come to save their brother from sickness and death, Jesus asks them to believe (John 11:21-23). But when he asks that they take away the stone from the tomb of Lazarus, who has now been dead for four days, Martha protests that there will be a stench. But Jesus responds, "Did I not tell you that if you would believe, you would see the glory of God?" (John 11:40). Jesus then thanks the Father for this glory which they will see, "Father, I thank you that you have heard me!" (John 11:41). His own death, too, will be for the greater glory of the Father: "Father, glorify your name!" (John 12:28).

So, too, in the spirituality of praise, we give glory to God in every situation. We praise him in all circumstances, no matter how painful these may be. For we believe that we shall see the glory of God at work in the situation. Just as the man was born blind not because he or his parents had sinned, "but that the works of God

123

might be made manifest in him" (John 9:3), so we believe that God's work will be manifest in every sickness or other suffering which we entrust to him in faith and love. "We know that in everything God works for good with those who love him, who are called according to his purpose" (Rom.8:28).

His purpose in every situation is to conform us to the image of his Son (Rom.8:29), making us like his Son in his paschal mystery, in which he comes to glory through loving obedience in sufferings. That is why the Christian praises God even in sufferings. "We rejoice in our hope of sharing the glory of God. More than that, we rejoice in our sufferings, knowing that suffering produces endurance, and endurance produces character, and character produces hope, and hope does not disappoint us, because God's love has been poured into our hearts through the Holy Spirit which has been given to us" (Rom.5:2-5).

The praise of God even in the most painful of situations is eloquent witness to our faith in the God of the new and eternal covenant, who is forever faithful to his promises. Absolute trust is the supreme witness to God's covenant love.

Not only is the raising of Lazarus a sign foreshadowing the Lord's own resurrection from death, but our Lord's attitude in the face of Lazarus's sickness and death reveals his attitude in the face of his own approaching death. He calmly stayed away and let Lazarus continue in his sickness till he died, even though he could have cured his sickness and saved him from death by his presence. So, too, he calmly goes to his own death, knowing that if he believes in his Father, he will see the glory of God (John 11:40). He knows that he can say of his own death what he has said about the man born

124

blind: he will suffer "so that the works of God might be made manifest in him" (John 9:3).

And just as he could give thanks to the Father for the raising of Lazarus while Lazarus still lay dead in the tomb, so he could praise God in the face of his own approaching death: "Father, I thank you that you have heard me" (John 11:41).

In instituting the Eucharist, "the sacrifice of praise," the night before he died, he is already praising God for his own death and resurrection, for he is already providing for our participation in his death and resurrection through the Eucharistic celebration. His absolute trust that the Father will vindicate him by raising him from death is itself already eloquent praise and thanksgiving rendered to the Father. In instituting "the sacrifice of praise" before his death, he is saying implicitly what he said concerning the dead Lazarus: "Father, I thank you that you have heard me. I know that you hear me always" (John 11:41-42). He knew that in his agony and death, the Father would hear his prayer.

St. John connects the prayer before the raising of Lazarus with the Eucharist, for he tells us that "Jesus *lifted up his eyes* and said, 'Father, I thank you that you have heard me'" (John 11:41). "Lifted up his eyes" is a Eucharistic formula. Likewise, John notes that Jesus lifted up his eyes (John 6:5) before feeding the five-thousand with five loaves, thus giving Eucharistic significance to that miraculous sign. "He lifted up his eyes to heaven" (John 17:1) is John's introduction to the prayer of Jesus at the Last Supper.

Thus, at the Last Supper, the Eucharist is the Lord's personal "sacrifice of praise" for his anticipated resurrection. It is his thanksgiving in advance for the resurrection and for all the fruits of his paschal sacrifice. He is already thanking the Father for all the benefits which will come to mankind through the Eucharistic celebration in the centuries to come. He witnesses to his conviction that these benefits will flow by making provision for their distribution through the Eucharist, the sacrifice of praise which he offers for his resurrection and for all its fruits in our lives.

Just as Jesus could have said to his Father in his prayer at the Last Supper, "I know that you always hear me," so we can do the same in all our troubles, knowing that when we love God and praise Him, the Lord and his Spirit are working in all things for our good (Rom.8:28).

The Eucharist: "The Sacrifice of Praise"

In Christian tradition through the centuries, the Eucharistic celebration has been called "the sacrifice of praise." The term occurs in the old Roman Canon (Eucharistic Prayer I), and also in the new preface for the Feast of Corpus Christi.* The Old Testament word for it was *todah* (Lev.7:12-15), which the Septuagint translated as "sacrifice of praise."

A *todah*, we have seen, was a sacrifice offered to God in thanksgiving for his favors. God was thanked not so much by saying, "Thank you, Lord," but by proclaiming

---

*Readers unfamiliar with Catholic liturgy may need some background. The Eucharistic celebration (the Lord's Supper) has two main parts: the Liturgy of the Word, consisting of Scripture readings, and the Liturgy of the Eucharist. The heart of this latter liturgy is the Eucharistic Prayer, containing the words and actions consecrating the Lord's Body and Blood. This prayer has the nature of a proclamation.

126

publicly at the sacrificial meal all the wonderful benefits God has granted to the person giving thanks. God's favors to the individual, however, were never seen in isolation. They were seen and acknowledged only in the context of God's total project of salvation. God was praised not simply for this gift or for that one, but for his whole magnificent work in carrying out all his purposes for his people.

The Eucharistic Prayer, the heart of the Eucharistic Liturgy, is a "sacrifice of praise" because it is a proclamation at a sacrificial meal of the wonderful works of God, praising him for what he has accomplished for us in the mystery of Jesus, sacrificed Lamb of God. It is a proclamation, moreover, that this Lamb is here and now present as risen Lord, forwarding God's saving purposes, working in us the fruits of his sacrifice.

God's whole purpose in all that he does throughout the universe is centered in Jesus: "He has made known to us . . . his purpose which he set forth in Christ as a plan for the fullness of time, to unite all things in him, things in heaven and things on earth" (Eph.1:9-10). We praise God for all of this in the proclamation at our sacrifice of praise, the Eucharistic Prayer. We glorify him for everything that he is doing for us in his Beloved Son "to the praise of his glorious grace which he freely bestowed on us in the Beloved" (Eph.1:6).

"Sacrifices of Acclamation"

Proclamation always calls for acclamation. In the Old Testament, the blowing of the trumpets on the great feasts was a proclamation of the presence of Yahweh with his people in the temple liturgy. To the trumpet call the people responded with the shout of acclamation, welcoming the Lord. Likewise, Mary's voice greeting Elizabeth was like the trumpet call, proclaiming that the Lord is here. Elizabeth responded with her loud cry of welcome to him and to his Mother.

So, too, in the Eucharistic celebration there is proclamation and acclamation. The Eucharistic prayer as a sacrifice of praise is a proclamation that the risen Lord is with us, accomplishing in us all the wonders of his paschal mystery. At various points in the great proclamation, the people respond with acclamations.

First, in the preface acclamation, we praise the three divine Persons, *Holy, Holy, Holy*, and we welcome the Lord Jesus in the cry *Hosanna!* Secondly, in the memorial acclamation after the consecration of the Lord's body and blood, we acclaim the Lord whose presence is proclaimed in the consecrated bread and wine. Thirdly, in the great *Amen* at the end of the Eucharistic Prayer, we respond to the whole proclamation of the Prayer and all its contents, and not simply to its concluding doxology.

Thus, the Eucharist, the sacrifice of praise, is also a sacrifice of acclamations. "I come to sacrifice in his tent sacrifices of acclamation" (Ps.26:6*b*). "Sacrifices of acclamation" (teruwah) has been variously translated as "sacrifice of jubilation," "sacrifices of joy," and "sacrifices with shouts of gladness" (*d,k,n*).

Let us consider these "shouts of gladness" offered to God by the Christian community in the Eucharistic celebration: the memorial acclamation at the consecration, the *Hosanna* in the preface acclamation, and the great *Amen* in response to the whole Eucharistic proclamation.

CHAPTER FIFTEEN

The Cup of Blessing

At the Last Supper, the night before he died, Jesus instituted the Eucharistic celebration by pronouncing a *berakah*, a table blessing.

In invoking a blessing upon men, the Jews always began by blessing God with words of praise: "Blessed are you, Lord, God of all creation. . . ." To bless God was to acknowledge him as the source of all blessings, the blessings of creation as well as those of salvation.

Israel was so certain that God is ever faithful to his covenant that she was convinced in faith that whenever God is praised and blessed, infallibly he pours forth the blessing which he is being asked to give. Thus, there is a power in the very words of blessing, for they are pronounced as a word of faith.

The Jewish Passover meal, at which the paschal lamb was eaten, began and ended with a *berakah*, a table blessing. The father of the family would take a loaf of bread, speak the blessing, break the bread, and give a piece of it to each one sitting at table, so that by eating the bread, each might share in the blessing on the meal.

After the meal, the father would speak the blessing over the cup, and would then pass the cup around so that by drinking of it all those at table would share in the blessing after the meal. Since the paschal meal was eaten in memory of the covenant which God made with his people when he brought them out of Egypt, all who ate the bread and drank from the cup shared in all the blessings of the covenant.

St. Paul clearly refers to the Eucharist as a *berakah*: "The cup of blessing which we bless, is it not a communion in the blood of Christ? The bread which we break, is it not a communion in the body of Christ? Because there is one bread, we who are many are one body, for we all partake of the one bread" (1 Cor.10:16-17).

At the Last Supper, in the setting of the old Jewish Passover, Jesus gave us the Eucharist as a *berakah*:

> On the night he was betrayed, he took bread and gave you thanks and praise. He broke the bread, gave it to his disciples and said: Take this, all of you, and eat it: this is my body which will be given up for you.
>
> When supper was ended, he took the cup. Again he gave you thanks and praise, gave the cup to his disciples and said: Take this, all of you, and drink from it: this is the cup of my blood, the blood of the new and everlasting covenant. It will be shed for you and for all men so that sins may be forgiven. Do this in memory of me.

(Eucharistic Prayer)

The Eucharistic words, given to us by the Lord as a *berakah*, infallibly call down the blessing of blessings: the risen Lamb himself, who was sacrificed for our sins, and who contains within himself all of God's blessings for mankind: "He who did not spare his own Son, but gave him up for us all, will he not also give us all things with him?" (Rom.8:32).

The Eucharistic blessing praises and blesses the God of the new and eternal covenant, the covenant which he sealed with us in the blood of the Lamb, his Son. In faithfulness to this covenant, the Almighty Father gives us the blessing asked for: the real presence here and now of the sacrificed and risen Lord Jesus, present as our loaf and cup of blessing, so that all who eat and drink of it will be in full communion with the Lord, sharing in his own communion with the Father in the Holy Spirit.

But to share in the Lord's communion with his Father, we must be in communion with him in his paschal mystery, his sacrificial death and resurrection. In the Scriptures, the cup symbolizes one's lot in life: "O Lord, my alloted portion and my cup, you it is who hold fast my lot" (Ps.16:5n). In the Eucharist, we share in the Lord's own cup; that is, we share in his lot in life, his God-given destiny. To drink the Lord's cup in the Eucharist is to share in his glory by sharing in his sufferings. For when James and John asked to share in his glory, he asked, "Can you drink the cup I shall drink or be baptized in the same bath of pain as I?" (Mark 10:38n). The Lord's lot or cup is glory reached through sufferings, and in this cup we share by partaking of the Eucharist.

Eucharistic Presence by the Power of the Word

All this comes to be because the Eucharist is a

berakah infallibly winning God's blessing, calling down the blessing of blessings, the risen Lamb himself. The word of blessing is the creative word of God. God's word is always creative. It calls into being what did not exist before. "By the word of the Lord the heavens were made. He spoke and (the earth) came to be" (Ps.33:6,9). The Lord God said, "Let there be light," and there was light! (Gen.1:3). The Lord Jesus said to the leper, "Be clean," and immediately the leprosy left him and he was made clean (Mark 1:41-42).

And the Lord said, "This is my body" (Mark 14:22), and therefore it *is* his body. He said, "This is my blood of the covenant" (Mark 14:24), and therefore it *is* his blood.

He said, "Do this in memory of me" (Luke 22:19), and by the power of these words, his apostles and their successors have the power to do what he did. In each Eucharistic celebration, the Lord Jesus himself speaks the creative words through the ministry of his priest: "This is my body; this is the cup of my blood." By the power of these words of proclamation and blessing, the risen Lord is infallibly present in the Eucharist as the blessing of blessings. For God speaks through his minister, the priest, and his word is accomplished.

In response to the proclamation of the Lord's word, "This is my body; this is the cup of my blood," we cry out our welcome to him in the memorial acclamation, for we know that he is present by the power of his word.

Since an acclamation is a cry of welcome to someone who is present, the acclamations after the consecration of the Lord's body and blood should be words addressed directly to the Lord, who is present through the power of the words of consecration. The acclamation should not be merely words about him, such as "Christ has died, Christ has risen, Christ shall come again." They should be words addressed directly to him, such as, "Dying, you destroyed our death, rising you restored our life, Lord Jesus! Come in Glory!" All the paradigm acclamations given in the official Latin text of the new missal are addressed directly to the Lord.

CHAPTER SIXTEEN

Hosanna!

"Hosanna to the Son of David! Blessed is he who comes in the name of the Lord! Hosanna in the highest!" (Matt.21:9). The Hebrew word "Hosanna!" has come untranslated into the Christian liturgy because the crowds on the first Palm Sunday greeted Jesus with this Hebrew acclamation as he entered the city of Jerusalem.

Hosanna! means "Grant salvation!" In using this word, the Palm Sunday crowds were quoting from Psalm 118: "O Lord, *grant salvation!* O Lord, grant prosperity! Blessed is he who comes in the name of the Lord" (Ps.118:25-26n). "Hosanna," as used in this psalm, was a victory cry. It was a celebration of salvation already granted. But why would a victory cry be expressed in terms of petition, "Grant salvation"?

The psalm in question was written to be sung at a *todah*, "a sacrifice of praise." This is evident from the psalm's stylized opening refrain, "Alleluia! (Proclaim) the Lord, for he is good, for his mercy endures forever!" (Ps.118:1n). Such *todah* psalms often dramatized the danger or the affliction from which the person had been saved and for which he was now giving thanks. His cry,

"O Lord, grant salvation," has been answered by the Lord, and, in the retelling of his affliction and of the deliverance from his affliction, the dramatization of his cry for help, "Hosanna," thus becomes a victory cry. As a cry of celebration, the Hebrew *Hosanna* remained untranslated even when the people no longer spoke Hebrew, but Aramaic. And so, too, it has passed untranslated into all languages.

This particular psalm was used on the Feast of Tabernacles. This feast celebrated the victories which "the outstretched arm of Yahweh" had won for his people in bringing them out of Egypt to the promised land and, later, in bringing them back to the land from exile in Babylon. In the celebration, branches were cut and carried in procession: "Join in procession with leafy boughs up to the horns of the altar" (Ps.118:27*n*). The branches themselves came to be called "hosannas" for they were symbols of God's victory over the foes of his people.

Tabernacles was a harvest festival, celebrated at the time of the ingathering of the grapes and olives in the fall of the year. God's gift of the promised land to his people was fittingly celebrated at the time when the fruits of that land were harvested. This feast of harvest joy was called "Abraham's joy," for God had kept his promise to Abraham, giving to his descendants this land whose fruits they were now enjoying. It was on the Feast of Tabernacles that Jesus proclaimed that he himself is Abraham's joy, for in his person all the promises made to Abraham find their most magnificent fulfillment: "Abraham rejoiced that he was to see my day; he saw it; and was glad" (John 8:56). Therefore to Jesus we cry, Hosanna!

Even while they were celebrating the salvation already granted, the hosannas—the cries and the upraised leafy boughs—were a petition for ongoing salvation. For in Israel the celebration of the salvation given in the past was always a pledge of continuing salvation in the present and in the future. To celebrate God's faithfulness to his covenant in the past was simultaneously to trust in his saving power here and now. The celebration itself and its victory cries were thus a petition for continuing salvation. So certain was God's faithfulness now and in the future that the very petition for his help—"Hosanna! Grant salvation!"—was already praise of God and joyous celebration of the salvation and victory still to be granted.

Thus, the word Hosanna is simultaneously a petition and a victory celebration, a lamentation and a cry of praise, and illustrates how closely lamentation and praise are related in the Hebrew psalter. So great is the trust in God expressed in a lamentation that the lamentation is already practically a thanksgiving.

Hosanna to the Risen Lord

When the people of Jerusalem on that first Palm Sunday cried out to Jesus, "Hosanna to the Son of David," Jesus knew that their cries expressed only half the truth. For even though he refused the demand of the chief priests that he forbid the children to give him the messianic title, "Son of David" (Matt.21:15-16), he denied that he was the kind of Messiah that the people wanted him to be. After receiving their hosannas, he proceeded to correct their false messianic notions (John

12:23-35). He began to speak of his coming death, and of himself as a suffering, spiritual Messiah, rather than a conquering earthly one. He referred to himself as the grain of wheat which must fall into the ground and die. He called himself the Son of Man who must be lifted up. "He said this to show by what death he was to die. The crowd answered him, 'We have heard from the law that the Christ remains forever. How can you say that the Son of Man must be lifted up? Who is this Son of Man?' " (John 12:33-34). They did not like the idea of a suffering Messiah which he presented to them. That was the beginning of their full rejection of him on the following Friday, when they themselves condemned him to be a crucified Messiah.

Thus, the true Hosanna is addressed only to the suffering and risen Lord, for only as obedient and suffering servant has he come into his glory as Son of God in power of salvation. To the risen Lord we cry, "Hosanna—grant salvation!"

Thus, some key words of the hosanna psalm take on a new and more profound meaning. "The stone which the builders rejected has become the cornerstone. By the Lord has this been done; it is wonderful in our eyes. This is the day which the Lord has made; let us be glad and rejoice in it" (Ps.118:22-24n). The day the Lord has made is the day of Jesus's resurrection.

The psalm originally celebrated the completion of the restoration of the temple after it had been destroyed by the Babylonians. When the Jews returned from the exile, Zerrubabel found the capstone of the temple buried in the rubble (Zech.4:6-7). In rebuilding the temple, he restored the stone to its place at the head of the corner (Zech.4:8-10). In the mind of the psalmist, however, the rejected and restored stone was a symbol of the chosen people of Israel, seemingly rejected by God at the time of the exile, but then brought back and restored by the faithful God. Thus, it became a cornerstone in the great work of restoring all mankind, building them all into a living temple of the true God (1 Pet.2:4-9).

After the resurrection of Jesus, the apostles quickly saw new meaning in the words of the psalm, and applied them to the Lord Jesus (Acts 4:11). Thus, the hosanna psalm has become the canticle par excellence of the Lord's resurrection: "This is the day which the Lord has made; let us be glad and rejoice in it!" (Ps.118:24n).

The Christian prayer of petition is always a hosanna of praise to the risen Lord, for to ask in his name is to ask in the power of his resurrection. It is to ask for all that he has won for us in that resurrection. It is to receive joyously all that has been given to us in him: "He who did not spare his own Son, but gave him up for us all, will he not also give us all things with him?" (Rom. 8:32). To ask whatever we will, in his name, is to praise the risen Lord.

The word, "Hosanna" thus reveals to us that Christian prayer of petition is simultaneously a prayer of praise, for one petitions the faithful God of the new covenant with such conviction of being heard that the very asking is already praise and thanksgiving; for all that is asked has already been granted in the Risen Lord.

So that all our asking will be with faith like that, it is well to begin our petitions with explicit praise of God and praise of his faithfulness to his covenant-love in raising Jesus from the dead. Such praise of his steadfast love is the proper setting for petition for his continuing help.

Charismatic Christians are well aware of this. Whenever, in the face of a need, one of them suggests, "Let's pray about it," immediately cries of "Alleluia! Praise you, Lord Jesus! Glory to the Lamb!" and the like burst forth. Then, in the setting of these cries of praise and acclamation of the Lord who is present, the petitions are expressed.

This, of course, has always been the approach in the official Catholic liturgy. In the liturgy of the hours, for example, which consists almost entirely of praise, petition is presented only after the singing of the psalms and hymns. The Eucharistic Liturgy, too, is predominantly a sacrifice of praise. It is the proclamation of the wonders God has accomplished for us in Jesus, the Paschal Lamb. Petition is expressed briefly in the Opening Prayer, the Prayers of the Faithful, the Prayer over the Gifts, and the Prayer after the Communion. Thus, only a fraction of the total time of the liturgy is given to petition, whereas the whole thrust of the Eucharistic Prayer is praise and acclamation.

Jesus Our Hosanna

If "Hosanna" means "Grant salvation," and "Jesus" means "Yahweh is salvation," then the name "Jesus" is the new hosanna. "Jesus" is the hosanna of praise and thanksgiving for salvation granted. At the same time it is petition for the continuing fruits of this salvation.

The name *Jesus* (in its full form *Yehosua*, or its contracted forms *Yosua* and *Yesua*) was rather common in the Old Testament times. As given in those days, the name was a prayer, an expression of faith in the saving power of God: "Yahweh is salvation." But in the case of the risen Lord Jesus, the name is no longer merely a prayer of petition. It expresses a truth of divine revelation. It is a statement of salvation already accomplished in Jesus: "Yahweh is salvation!" It is a hosanna of both praise and petition.

Salvation is already fully accomplished in the person of Jesus, for he was exalted in glory because of his obedience unto death. And the profession "Jesus is Lord" is a hosanna summing up all praise: "At the name of Jesus, every knee should bow, in heaven and on the earth and under the earth, and every tongue confess that Jesus Christ is Lord, to the glory of God the Father" (Phil.2:10-11).

In the preface acclamation in the Eucharistic celebration, the "Hosanna" does not stand alone. It is part of an acclamation addressed to the Holy Trinity in words taken from Isaiah's great vision of Yahweh: "Holy, holy, holy Lord God of hosts!" (cf., Isa.6:3). The thrice Holy One is the Yahweh who is our salvation, and this salvation is given to us only in Jesus, his Son.

Thus, the Hosanna addressed to Jesus in the Eucharistic celebration finds its full meaning only within the "Holy, holy, holy," the acclamation addressed to the three divine Persons. Yahweh is salvation in and through Jesus, for Jesus is Savior only by the will of the Father and through the cooperation of the Holy Spirit. "Lord Jesus Christ, Son of the living God, by the will of the Father and the work of the Holy Spirit, your death brought life to the world."[42]

This salvation is ever present among us, fully manifest and operative in the risen Lord Jesus, and is in process of being communicated to us. It is all contained in him, and is working from him in us through the Holy Spirit whom he gives to us.

Thus the name "Jesus," our hosanna, is our joyful prayer of acceptance of this salvation. "There is salvation in no one else, for there is no other name under heaven given among men by which we must be saved" (Acts 4:12).

Just to cry out *"Jesus!"* as a lamentation and petition from the midst of distress is at the same time to praise the Lord and to thank him for the expected deliverance. The very petition is praise, for it is the grateful claiming of the life and salvation already present and offered in Jesus.

Using his name in faith means accepting his healing power, the power to heal hearts, the power to heal bodies, the power to heal human relationships. God is glorified by these wonders done in the name of his Son. "Did I not tell you that if you believe, you would see the glory of God?" (John 11:40).

What better way of praising God is there than accepting with confidence the salvation he offers, claiming all that is promised in that name, using all the power which works in that name? The faith which works wonders in the name of Jesus is magnificent praise of God. Believing is receiving. Believing is accepting him at his word, and claiming the wonders which he wills to perform through faith in his name.

If the leafy branches, the symbols of victory carried in the processions on the Feast of Tabernacles, were called hosannas, Jesus himself is our Hosanna, whom we offer to the Father in the Eucharist, the perfect sacrifice of praise.

CHAPTER SEVENTEEN

Amen!

In the Eucharistic celebration, the people listen to "the sacrifice of praise"—the proclamation of the paschal mystery of Jesus—and they respond with "sacrifices of acclamation," especially the great *Amen!*

An acclamation implies the presence of the one acclaimed. In this case, it is the presence of the risen Lord, "the Lamb standing as if slain" (Rev.5:6), risen from death yet always bearing in his body his wounds. He is ever living in our midst, producing in us the fruits of his sacrifice. To acclaim the Lord is to receive him with joy and to accept the salvation he brings. This we do in the Eucharistic Amen.

The Hebrew word *Amen!* (So be it!), derives from a verb meaning to confirm, to uphold; which in turn derives from a root meaning to be steadfast, trustworthy. *Amen* was used to confirm the truth of a statement. It was used to give assent to an administered oath (Neh. 5:13; Jer.11:5), to signify agreement with a good wish (1 Kings 1:36; Jer.28:6), to accept a blessing and to ratify a prayer (1 Chron.16:36). Thus, in the liturgy of the synagogues, the people made the prayer of their leader their own by answering, "Amen!" The early Christians continued the same practice: "If your praise of God is solely with the spirit, how will the one who does not comprehend be able to say 'Amen' to your thanksgiving?" (1 Cor.14:16n).

Amen therefore means: I set my seal to that! I accept and confirm it. Not only does my Amen means "It is so!" It means also "So be it!" Not only does it mean, "It is true!" It means also, "May it become true in me!"

Proclamation of the New Covenant

What do we accept and confirm in the Amen to the Eucharistic Prayer? We accept and ratify everything that is proclaimed in that prayer. Especially, the Eucharistic Amen is our faith accepting the truth proclaimed at the heart of that prayer:

> On the night he was betrayed, he took bread and gave you thanks and praise. He broke the bread, gave it to his disciples and said: Take this, all of you, and eat it: this is my body which will be given up for you.
>
> When supper was ended, he took the cup. Again he gave you thanks and praise, gave the cup to his disciples and said: Take this, all of you, and drink from it: this is the cup of my blood, the blood of the new and everlasting covenant. It will be shed for you and for all men, so that sins may be forgiven.

Such are the words and actions which make the Eucharist truly a *todah*, a sacrifice of praise. In these words and actions at a meal, Jesus praises and glorifies God by giving witness to the Father's love for the world. He proclaims the good news of peace and reconciliation in his own blood. He proclaims the new and eternal covenant in that blood. "For as often as you eat this bread and drink this cup, you proclaim the Lord's death until he comes" (1 Cor.11:26).

Our Amen is our response to this proclamation of the good news. It is our ratification of the covenant: *So be it!* We set our seal to the new and eternal covenant, we assent to it and assume the responsibilities it proposes to us, and we eat his body and drink his blood in celebration of this. Our Amen is the meeting of our Yes with God's Yes, in one Yes. And that Yes is Jesus.

Jesus, the Yes!

Amen means *Yes!* St. Paul says, "All the promises of God find their Yes in Jesus Christ. That is why we utter the Amen through him, to the glory of God" (2 Cor.1: 19-20). The great Amen in response to the Eucharistic Prayer is best explained in the light of these words of St. Paul.

The Eucharistic Prayer proclaims that "all of God's promises find their Yes in Jesus;" that is, all of God's promises are fulfilled in him. They are fulfilled in Jesus because Jesus said *Yes!* to the Father, and thus was perfectly open to what God willed to accomplish in him and through him for us. His words, "Not my will, but yours, be done" (Luke 22:42) are his great Amen, his *So be it!* Jesus himself is the Amen, because he is the Yes to God for us. He is the perfect response to God's will

144

announced in his promises. Through this Yes, God was able to fulfill his promises.

Thus, all of God's promises find their fulfillment in Jesus because of his wholehearted Yes to the purposes of God's love. "That is why we utter the Amen through him, to the glory of God." In saying Amen to Jesus, we make his Yes to God our own.

In saying Yes, Jesus gave glory to God by accepting salvation for all mankind. In response to this Yes of Jesus, the Father poured out the fullness of the promised Spirit upon the risen Jesus, so that Jesus in turn might communicate this Holy Spirit to us. Thus, Jesus is God's Yes to us, for he contains in himself, for us, all that God has poured out in fulfillment of his promises.

The Eucharistic Prayer proclaims this good news. He who says Amen to this proclamation "sets his seal to this, that God is true" (John 3:33). He has been true to his word, he has fulfilled all that he has spoken through the prophets. He has been true to his own Amen in sealing the covenant with Abraham and his descendants. And he is being true to his word here and now, for he is present here and now in the Eucharistic Jesus, offering to us all that he has promised. All the promises of God are here and now finding their Yes among us in the Eucharistic Jesus, who is present with us, pouring out his gifts to us when we say Yes to him, just as he said Yes to the Father. We express this Yes in the Amen to the Eucharistic proclamation. Our Yes, like the Yes of Jesus, gives praise to God, for to accept his gifts with appreciation is to praise and glorify him.

The Amen is Praise and Petition

The Eucharistic Prayer, then, is a proclamation that the Lord is here with us as the fulfillment of all of God's promises. And the Amen to this proclamation is an acclamation: a welcoming of the Lord Jesus and an accepting of his gifts. The Amen is our acceptance of the Promise, it is our Yes to God's plans of love for us, it is our openness in desire for his blessings, it is our Yes to the Holy Spirit and his gifts offered to us in Jesus, it is petition for all that he wills to give us. In all these ways, the Amen is an eloquent word of praise.

The Amen is the best petition, and it is the best praise. It is petition, because it expresses the desire of our heart for all that is proclaimed in God's word and in the Eucharistic Prayer. It is the best petition I could offer to God, for it is a desiring and asking and accepting of all that he wants to do for me in Christ. And it is the best praise, for my *So be it* subordinates my own desires and petitions to the proclaimed purposes of God's love. This is to praise his wisdom in preference to my own.

All truly Christian petition is an Amen to God's wisdom proclaimed in his word. Our petition is a "be it done to me according to your word" (Luke 1:38). For Jesus says, "If you abide in me, and my words abide in you, ask whatever you will, and it shall be done for you" (John 15:7). When his word abides in me, it inspires all my desires and petitions. I desire only what his word proclaims, only what his word promises. Thus my desires and petitions are the best possible, for they are educated by God's word to focus on the most desirable of all gifts, the glorious gifts which God's love

146

chooses to give us in Christ. To appreciate and ask for these gifts is to praise God.

That is why the Amen at the end of the Eucharistic Prayer is an Amen also to the Liturgy of the Word, which proclaims what the Lord wills to do in us by the power of the Eucharist. Hence, the great importance of the ministry of the word, and especially the homily on the word. The desires and petitions of God's people need to be educated to expect the very best that God has to offer.

The word Amen at the end of the Eucharistic Prayer is but the verbal expression of an attitude in response, of acceptance, and of praise which should be building up in the hearts of the people as the Eucharistic celebration proceeds.

Our Amen is a wholehearted entering into the Lord's own sacrifice of praise, for in the Eucharistic Prayer, Jesus is present proclaiming all the wonders that God has accomplished in him for us: "This is my body, which is given up *for you*; this is my blood, which is shed *for you*." To say Amen to this is to praise and thank God with Jesus, the Yes in whom God gives us everything. "That is why we utter the Amen through him, to the glory of God" (2 Cor.1:20). "Through him, with him, in him, in the unity of the Holy Spirit, all honor and glory is yours, Almighty Father, for ever and ever! AMEN!"

CHAPTER EIGHTEEN

Believing Is Praising

The Amen to the Eucharistic Prayer is a summary of the faith which is called forth by every element in the liturgy. It is our faith putting its seal of approval and acceptance upon all that is proclaimed.

The total Gospel is proclaimed in the Eucharist, for the Eucharist proclaims Jesus who is the Gospel. In giving his life for us, Jesus is the Gospel in action. In giving us his body and blood in the Eucharist, the risen Jesus is the Gospel in action here and now, proclaiming and communicating to us reconciliation with God and the fullness of life in him.

Our faith is our Amen accepting all of this. Faith is receiving what we believe. Believing is receiving. "To as many as received him, by believing in his name, he gave the power to become sons of God" (John 1:12d). To believe is to receive the Son of God, and the gift of divine sonship in him. But this is to praise God, for to accept his love is to praise him.

The praise expressed in the Amen admits of various degrees of perfection. The first degree is merely believing the truth proclaimed and lovingly admiring God's love expressed in his plan of wisdom. My Amen is my faith assenting to the truth: *It is so!*

A higher degree of praise in my Amen is my *Be it so!* This is my hearty desire and petition for the implementation of what I believe. For to desire ardently that God's plan be implemented to the full is greater praise than simply to admire the plan. If I did not love the plan so much that I ardently desired its fulfillment, my admiration of the plan would seem to lack sincerity. If someone offered me a beautiful precious gift, and I praised it—saying, "Oh how beautiful, how precious!"—but then walked off without wanting and accepting it, would not my words, "How precious," sound false? The most sincere praise of God's wisdom is therefore desire for and acceptance of the love and gifts he offers in his wisdom. Praise springs from appreciation. To appreciate God's blessings is to desire and accept them. Therefore my Amen is not perfect praise unless it is a wholehearted *Yes: Be it done to me!* My Amen is my *hope* eagerly desiring and expecting and accepting God's active wisdom into my life.

A still more intense degree of praise in my Amen is the *Yes!* which expects God to do his wonders in me in a truly magnificent way. "Lord, you have been doing such glorious things in me! What new marvels are you going to accomplish in me today? I am ready for them all! Glorify your name!" Such a Yes to his love beautifully praises and glorifies God, for it witnesses to the greatness of his love which is so eager to do marvels in all of us; and he never goes back on his promise to do them. The only hindrance to his loving generosity is our indifference to him.

St. Paul's expectant Yes! was expressed in his great

doxology: "Now to him who by the power at work within us is able to do far more abundantly than all that we ask or think, to him be glory in the church and in Christ Jesus to all generations, for ever and ever! *Amen!*" (Eph.3:20-21).

To doubt God's loving eagerness to do wonders in us is just the opposite of praise. It is the sin of pusilanimity, the petty meanness, the narrowness of heart, which will not open the heart to aspire to great things for the glory of God. But magnanimity is the true Amen. Magnanimity is the greatness of heart which is fully open to God's magnificent purposes, and accepts the full responsibility which comes with receiving his wonderful blessings. It takes courage to say *Yes!* to God's love, which always asks very great things of those whom he chooses. Only magnanimous generosity can give a full Amen to God's call.

That is why his call is always accompanied by a "Fear not! You have found grace with God" (Luke 1:30d). The more we expect from God's love, the more we honor and praise him.

My most eloquent Amen of praise, my most intense degree of praise, is my living the Amen in all of my life, in such a way that my life becomes an *Amen! Alleluia!* in the Amen which is Christ's own life. This is doing "the truth in love" (Eph.4:15). This is the Amen which uncompromisingly accepts the wisdom of the cross into my life, the wisdom which is proclaimed and offered to me in the Eucharist: "This is my body, given up for you; this is my blood, shed for you; *do this in memory of me.*" That is, do what I have done, by the power of this body and blood. Say Amen to the cross in your life, by loving your brothers and sisters as I have loved you, at the cost of death to self.

Thus, my Amen to the Eucharistic proclamation is not only an act of faith in the truth of the Lord's gift of his body and blood to me in the Eucharist, it is a ready acceptance of that body and blood into my whole life. I fully accept his body and blood only when I accept the power and Spirit they contain for me. And in this power and Spirit I make my whole life an Amen of praise in that of Jesus.

The Body of Christ! Amen!

In the communion rite of the Mass, too, there is a proclamation and an acclamation: the proclamation—"The Body of Christ!"; the acclamation in response—"Amen!"

This Amen is not merely a profession of faith in the truth of the proclamation. It is also the believing which is receiving. It is an acclamation welcoming the risen Lord in person, who is giving himself to me in his body and blood. It is *Be it so!* to all that the Eucharistic Lord wills to do in all those who receive him in expectant faith. It is a Yes to all that was proclaimed in the liturgy of the word and in the Eucharistic Prayer. For what the Lord proclaimed in these ways he accomplishes in those who eat his flesh and drink his blood in expectant faith and hope. Our Yes is the door to him and to all that he wills to do in us.

Personal Witness

As I distribute the Body and Blood of Christ to God's people in the communion rite, in confirmation of their

151

Amen I find myself saying *Alleluia!* in my heart. My wholehearted *Alleluia!* is a kind of overflowing of their *Amen*. It is a petition to the Lord to fulfill in this person before me all the promises contained in this gift of his body. As I place the Lord's body on the recipient's tongue, my *Alleluia* means something like this: "Praise you, Lord Jesus! May this tongue bless you, and may this person's life glorify you and your Father!"

I am the Lord's minister, and therefore the desire of his heart must become mine, his prayer must be expressed in mine. I bring not only his body and blood, but also his love which wills to be frutiful in all who receive him. His love in my heart prays for those to whom I minister his body and blood. His prayer in my heart make his body and blood all the more fruitful in those to whom I give it, for my love is an added way in which he is present to them. Only with love like this in my heart am I a fitting minister of the Lord's Eucharist.

The Continuing Amen

The Amen to the Eucharistic Prayer, and the Amen with which we receive the Lord's Body, are expressed in a flash. And yet in this flash, through a mere *Yes!*, the Lord can work marvels in a heart.

The ardor of this Yes in a flash, however, can come to its full fervor only when it has been aroused and nourished by a moving liturgy of the word, by a sincere and thoughtful proclamation of the Eucharistic Prayer, and by all the singing and expressions of praise which surround the whole Eucharistic Action—the entrance song, the responsorial psalm, the preface acclamation with its hosannas, the communion songs, and the recessional singing.

When all of this is done in true spiritual fervor, the joyous melody of the *Amen! Alleluia!* will continue to resound in the hearts of the participants as they go forth to their work or to their rest. "Be filled with the Spirit. Sing the words and tunes of the psalms and hymns when you are together, and go on singing and chanting to the Lord in your hearts, so that always and everywhere you are giving thanks to God who is our Father, in the name of our Lord Jesus Christ" (Eph.5:18-20j). Amen! Alleluia!

CHAPTER NINETEEN

The "Amen" to Preaching

All preaching of God's word, like the Eucharistic Prayer, is a proclamation of the paschal mystery, calling for an *Amen!* Preaching is praise of God, and so is the Amen to it.

Preaching is praise, for it is the public proclamation of the wonderful works which God has accomplished in his Son, Jesus, and is a declaration also that he wills to continue and complete these wonders here and now in those who hear the word and accept it. The listeners' Amen to this proclamation is praise, for it is loving appreciation of what God has proclaimed and is eager petition for the implementation of this in our lives.

St. Paul says that preaching is a spiritual liturgy: "I worship (God) in the spirit by preaching the gospel of his Son" (Rom.1:9n). All worship and liturgy is essentially praise, for it is acknowledgment of the perfections of God our Savior. In this liturgy of preaching, the minister of the word offers men to God; or more exactly, Christ offers men to God through this ministry: "God has given me the grace to be a minister of Christ Jesus among the Gentiles, with the priestly duty of

154

preaching the gospel of God so that the Gentiles may be offered up as a pleasing sacrifice, consecrated by the Holy Spirit" (Rom.15:15-16n). Men effectively rise to God as a spiritual sacrifice only through their willing response, their *Amen*, to the word which is preached.

Not only is preaching itself praise, but all genuine preaching is rooted in praise. For I cannot say truthfully that "I worship God in my spirit when I preach," unless in the Holy Spirit I have experienced the truth of the message I preach and have praised God for it at least by my interior Amen, my interior joy and appreciation of the Lord and his truth.

The Acts of the Apostles shows that the original apostles first praised God, and only then preached. "They were all filled with the Holy Spirit, and began to speak in other tongues, as the Spirit gave them utterance" (Acts 2:4). The crowd's response showed that in these tongues the apostles were singing praises of God: "We hear them telling in our own tongues the mighty works of God" (Acts 2:11). This praising in all languages was a symbol and anticipation of the mission to preach to all nations. When they preached to others, the apostles were proclaiming what they had already sung in praise to God. Every preacher needs to root his preaching in such praise of God.

What we are saying in this chapter about formal preaching of the word of God is true also of other forms of the ministry of the word, in a proportionate way. It is true of all such word-gifts as the inspired reading of passages from the word of God, prophecy, teaching and the like, as these are exercised in charismatic prayer meetings. In these ways, too, people can speak in Spirit and in power. All these forms of ministry of the word should evoke an Amen in response.

155

Personal Witness

In a remarkable way I have experienced the power of praise in its relationship with preaching and teaching and other exercise of the word-gifts. Recently, for example, along with a religious sister I was conducting a workshop for religious men and women at a charismatic conference. In the charismatic renewal, it is customary always to praise God before preaching or teaching. Therefore, sister and I spent some time together in praise and in petition before going to the auditorium where we were to speak. When we arrived there, we found that our audience had been beautifully prepared to hear our word, for the music ministry had been leading the assembled people in singing God's praises. Thus their hearts were opened to hear God's word.

When we began to speak, the song leaders continued to bless the Lord silently in their hearts, for they had been commissioned to continue to pray that God would pour out his blessing through our ministry of the word. The sister spoke first, and while she was speaking, I too was filled with the praise of God—a silent interior praise in my heart, which nonetheless bubbled to my lips and caused them to move silently in praise. My praise was also petition, for I was blessing God so that he would bless the speaker and the listeners. I was praying that they would be moved by the word and would glorify God by accepting it into their lives.

Sister spoke like a prophet, proclaiming in confident and undoubting faith that God would accomplish in the lives of her audience those things which she was proclaiming, if they would only say *Yes* to what he was announcing through her word, if they would say *Amen* to what she was proclaiming as God's purpose for them. The *Yes* which she was calling forth from the hearts of her listeners amounted to a complete and loving surrender of self to the Lord for the accomplishment of his plan. "God will do this in your life if you say 'Yes' to him!"

She could proclaim her message with such boldness because she had received it in much prayer and reflection upon the Scriptures, in the consciousness of the condition and needs of her audience. In this prayer and reflection she had not been alone, but had been supported by a community of sisters with whom she prayed regularly, who had joined her in her petition for the word she was to speak.

When it was my turn to speak, I could hear sister behind me quietly and earnestly praising Jesus. I strongly experienced her praise as a power supporting me as I spoke. One especially moving and helpful aspect of this was her sincere and emphatic *Amen!* to my various points as I made them. Her Amen was so soft that only I could hear it, yet it was full of power and Spirit. It was not only her heartfelt seal of approval on what I was saying: *It is so!* It was also her ardent petition that the Lord would bring these truths to fulfillment in the lives of those who were listening: *Be it so!* Lord Jesus, bring it to be in their hearts and in their lives.

Later reflection on this vivid experience brought me to understand and to write all that I have written in the preceding chapters about the great Eucharistic Amen. It also brought to mind how Lacordaire, the great Dominican preacher of the nineteenth century, used to say that his preaching was fruitful only because his companion, a Dominican brother, was always praying behind the altar while he preached. The experience helped me to appreciate more deeply than ever the role of the cloistered Dominican nuns, whose lives of divine praise bring fruitfulness to the work of their preaching brothers.

Another fruit of this experience was a new way of preaching which began to develop in me after this. More and more I began to find myself saying emphatically at the end of my homilies such things as: "This is what God's word proclaims in today's liturgy, so this is what he wills to give you this day. Accept it!" "What I have spoken is what the Lord wills to do in you! Say Amen to it! Let him do it!" "When I reflected upon the word of this liturgy, this is what God inspired me to preach. Therefore, this is what he wills to form in your hearts by his Spirit and power. Say *Yes* to him." Moreover, I frequently say: "The Lord will accomplish all of this in you by the power of this Eucharistic sacrifice, through his body and blood which he will give to you in this celebration."

Preaching in Spirit and in Power

Every preacher must be convinced that it is his mission to proclaim what the Lord wills to do in those who hear him. He must inspire faith in this proclamation. He must stir up the believing which is receiving, receiving the Lord and the specific work he wills to accomplish this day in the hearers of the word.

When the Lord wills to do something in the hearts of believers, through his Holy Spirit he inspires a desire for what he intends to do, and this desire opens the heart to receive it. "He who searches the hearts of men knows what is the mind of the Spirit, because the Spirit intercedes for the saints according to the will of God" (Rom. 8:27). That is, the Spirit opens the heart of the believer to desire and to ask for what God wills to accomplish in him. The Spirit uses preachers especially to inspire this desire for what he wills to give. "Indeed, the Lord does nothing without revealing his plan to his servants, the prophets" (Amos 3:7n).

The Amen to the preached word is the Spirit-inspired desire and petition for what the preacher has proclaimed. He proclaims only what truly is God's plan and will for these listeners. An Amen to such preaching springs spontaneously from the joy experienced when God touches the heart: It is so! Be it so!

This is what is meant by preaching in Spirit and power (1 Cor.2:4, 1 Thess.1:5). We must be convinced that God proclaims in the liturgy of the word what he wills to do in the hearts of those who are listening. Even as we preach, we should be convinced that his power and Spirit is announcing what he wills to do.

Preachers should encourage their listeners to respond with a sincere vocal Amen. For their response to the word should not be some vague, unexpressed wish that all this might perhaps come true in their hearts. It should be an explicit, ardent, expectant *Amen!* expressing the conviction that God does will to do this. "Yes, I have spoken, I will accomplish it; I have planned it, and I will do it!" (Isa.46:11n).

The preacher should present his message with that conviction, the conviction that God does will to do these things which he proclaims. He should take care to discern just what God does will to do in his people, and proclaim only this. Such discernment is possible only in deep faith and prayer and persistent reflection on God's word. This prayer and reflection should be expectant openness to God's grace, which will give him the word he is to preach.

This word must spring also from the preacher's loving concern for God's people and from a keen awareness of their needs and problems. But he looks at these needs and problems as a listener to God. When St. Dominic prayed with tears, night after night, saying, "Lord, what is to become of the sinners?" he was not only *praying* for the sinners, he was asking what he personally should *do* about them, and what he should preach to touch their hearts.

I Will Open My Ear

The preacher's prophetic function in the face of the people's problems is well illustrated in Psalm 49. The theme of the psalm springs from the poet's personal experience of a universal problem: why the wicked seem to prosper, while the just seem only to suffer. He considers the problem in the presence of God, listening for a word of solution from the Lord: "I will incline my ear to a proverb" (Ps.49:4), a saying which will sum up the Lord's answer. I will open my ear to receive a striking way of putting the answer, a memorable phrase which will sink deep into the hearts of my hearers and will strike root and bear fruit.

The author of this psalm was a teacher, who first learned to hear what he teaches! And his answer comes, perhaps, in the midst of anointed singing: "I will solve my riddle to the music of the lyre" (Ps.49:4). Once

160

when the prophet Elisha was seeking an answer from God, he called for a sacred minstrel to play, to open his heart to the Spirit of God. The Lord's word came while the minstrel played and sang (2 Kings 3:15).

In the midst of anointed praise of God, the Holy Spirit gives light to solve the riddles of life. This can happen especially when a whole group is seeking the answer together, in praise and prayer. A week or so before I wrote this, for example, I met with the leaders of a charismatic community who were seeking practical decisions in facing important problems. As is usual when these men meet for making decisions, they began by praising God. They continued in profound prayer for fifty-five minutes before the presiding leader called them to the consideration of the problems.

This is the normal way for charismatic leaders to approach decisions. Such an approach to practical life problems is bound to bear fruitful answers.

All preaching, teaching and pastoral direction should be rooted in community prayer of this sort, if it is to be fully fruitful in the hearts of God's people. Every Christian parish should have its prayer group with whom the leaders of the parish, especially the pastor, should meet to pray before making pastoral decisions. Out of such community prayer, too, should come all preaching. Jesus made the fruits of the apostolate fully dependent upon our asking for them: "I chose you and appointed you that you should go and bear fruit and that your fruit should abide; so that whatever you *ask* the Father in my name, he may give it to you" (John 15:16).

The preacher should be a harp ever attuned to the Spirit of God, who gives him the song he is to sing, the words he is to preach.

The Vocal Amen To The Word

If the preacher's proclamation of the word is effective, the desire for its fulfillment will be stirred up in the hearts of the listeners. And if this desire is expressed aloud in such words as "Amen! Alleluia!" it will be deepened into undoubting faith and expectant hope. The "Alleluia!" (Praise the Lord!) is an acclamation of welcome to the Lord who is present to do what he has just spoken. The "Amen" means "Be it done to me according to your word!" (Luke 1:38). Such exclamations are a prayer of conviction for the accomplishment of what the Lord has spoken through his preacher. They are words of appreciation and acceptance of what the Lord's love wills to do.

Our people need to be freed from the inhibitions which keep them from expressing such expectant faith. They are inhibited by a weakness of faith, which is weak because it is not expressed often enough in this expectant way. Their faith is weak because they have not yet realized that faith is not faith until I am convinced that it concerns me personally! God has spoken to *me*! Christ loves *me*, and delivered himself up for me personally (cf.,Gal.2:20).

And even when our people believe in their hearts, they are inhibited by a fear of expressing their faith aloud, and so do not benefit by the growth and deepening of faith which comes in its exterior profession: "If you confess with your lips that Jesus is Lord and believe in your heart that God raised him from the dead, you will be saved!" (Rom.10:9). When faith is characterized by the joy of love and expectancy, it wants to cry out

162

Amen! Alleluia! each time the Lord speaks, whether in the liturgy of the word, or in the Eucharistic Prayer, or in any other way.

The charismatic *Amen! Alleluia!* is not sheer emotion. It is the spiritual joy which accompanies what St. Paul calls *parrhesia*, the daring confidence of the children of God, who have free access to their Father in the Spirit of Jesus and expect great things from him as they welcome the Lord Jesus in trusting faith. "In Christ Jesus our Lord, through faith in him, we have boldness and confidence of access to God" (Eph.3:11-12). Who can fail to rejoice in the Lord's presence and to acclaim him with love? Can we remain in frozen silence when we realize this glorious truth? If we never care to shout out with joy to the Lord, perhaps we have never tasted his truth.

Of course, if I say *Amen! Alleluia!* to God's word, but do nothing about living it, the praise contained in that Amen proves to be sounding brass and tinkling cymbal. But a life lived in accordance with that word and by the power of that word is a beautiful Amen to God's glory. Such a life is the truest praise. Such a life comes about, however, only if in faith and love we say Amen to God's word and liturgy.

Our whole life, says St. Paul, is to be praise of God's glory: "We have been destined and appointed to live for the praise of his glory" (Eph.1:12). A life which is praise is filled with joy. The joy bursts forth in words and songs of praise, expressing the life which is praise. *Laus Gloriae*, "the praise of his glory" (Eph.1:6,12,14), should be every Christian's name.

163

Personal Witness

More and more of late I have had the joy of hearing a heartfelt *Amen!* spring spontaneously from the lips of some of those who listen to my preaching of the word. This has been true, of course, only in so-called "charismatic" audiences—people who are not hampered by the fear of expressing what is in their hearts. These people can therefore grow spiritually, because they deepen what is in their hearts by expressing it sincerely and emphatically, in word, song, or even dance, as circumstances permit.

At times I have heard applause in response to the Spirit-filled preaching of my colleagues. Rather than the clapping of hands, however, I would prefer cries of "Amen! Alleluia! Praise the Lord! Thanks be to God!" Handclapping can be ambiguous. The preacher can interpret it too easily as praise of himself rather than praise of the Lord. But explicit words addressed to the Lord, "Amen! Glory! Alleluia!" will give the praise where it is due—to the Lord. "This is the Lord's doing; it is marvelous in our eyes!" (Ps.118:23).

CHAPTER TWENTY

Lauda Sion!

"We say much, yet fall short in our words. But the sum of all our words is 'He is all!' " (Sir.43:29*d*). Thus, the Scriptures speak of the hopelessness of our efforts to praise God enough. Yet the very greatness of the One whom we cannot praise adequately is the reason why we should praise him to the maximum of our ability:

> Glorify the Lord with all your power, for he will yet far exceed, and his magnificence is wonderful. Blessing the Lord, exalt him as much as you can, for he is above all praise. When you exalt him, put forth all your strength and be not weary, for you can never go far enough (Sir.43:32-34*d*).

Yet the Lord God in his magnificence has found a way for his creatures to praise him adequately. In the Eucharist, "the sacrifice of praise," he has given us his Son's infinite praise as our own, to offer it to the glory of the Father: "Through him, with him, in him, in the unity of the Holy Spirit, all glory and honor is yours, Almighty Father, for ever and ever! Amen!"

To help God's people to celebrate the feast of Corpus Christi, the solemn festival of the Lord's Body and Blood, St. Thomas Aquinas composed a sequence for the Mass. Thomas begins by echoing the words of Sirach which we have just quoted, and calls upon us to praise Jesus for all his works, but most especially for the gift of the Eucharist:

> Zion, praise your Savior! Praise your leader and shepherd in hymns and canticles! Praise him as much as you can, for he is beyond all praising, and you will never be able to praise him as he deserves. But today a theme worthy of particular praise is put before us: the living and life-giving Bread that was truly given to the Twelve at table during the holy supper.
>
> Therefore let our praise be full and resounding, and our soul's rejoicing full of delight and splendor, for this is the festival day to commemorate the first institution of the new King's table.

The Lord's giving of the Eucharist to us is not only a most special reason for praising God, but as we are told in the new preface for the feast of Corpus Christi, the Eucharist itself is perfect praise: "At the Last Supper, as he sat at table with his apostles, he offered himself to you, Father, as the spotless Paschal Lamb, the perfect sacrifice of praise." In giving us the Eucharist, the Lord has given us his own perfect praise of God so that we might offer it as our own.

The sacrifice of Jesus is absolutely perfect praise in itself both because of the infinite worth of him who offers it—God's own Son, whose dignity equals that of his Father—and because of the perfect dispositions of his heart and soul in offering it. On the cross, Jesus fulfilled to perfection the greatest of the commandments: "You shall love the Lord your God with all your heart, and with all your soul, and with all your mind, and with all your strength, and your neighbor as yourself" (cf., Mark 12:33).

For there was no greater love than Christ's in laying down his life for his brothers (John 15:13). And this he did in perfect love of the Father, "so that the world may know that I love the Father" (John 14:31). This was perfect praise, for such love witnesses adequately to the Father's love for him and for all mankind: "As the Father has loved me, so have I loved you" (John 15:9). I have responded to the Father's love for me by loving him in return, and I have expressed this love for him by loving you in giving my life for you. No greater testimony to the God of love could be given.

The love was perfect, and the dignity of the Lover was infinite, and so our Lord's praise was equal to the dignity of the God whom he praised. He himself, the spotless Lamb sacrificed for the glory of the Father, is the perfect sacrifice of praise.

In the Eucharist he has given us this sacrifice of praise to be our own, so that "through him, with him, in him" we can give perfect praise, "uttering the Amen through him, to the glory of God" (2 Cor.1:20).

The Eucharist is not simply a matter of our standing outside of Jesus and watching him offer perfect praise to the Father on our behalf. It is a matter of our entering into the perfect praise of Jesus, becoming one with it, making it our own through our identity with Jesus and with his dispositions in offering himself.

In the actual offering of the Eucharist we are identified with Jesus through faith and love. But this unity with him in the liturgical offering is for the sake of an ever more perfect oneness with him in the totality of our life. His sacrifice of perfect praise becomes most truly our own to the extent that his own life, the great Amen, is fashioned in us by the power of the Eucharist.

We have entered into his perfect praise, and his praise has become truly our own, when we can say Amen to our life in the way that he said Amen to his, when we can glorify the Father in every life-situation in the way that he glorified the Father every day in every way: "I always do what is pleasing to him" (John 8:29).

Our *life* thus becomes a sacrifice of praise, not only in the likeness of the Lord's sacrifice, but his sacrifice becomes ours and ours becomes his, for our life is lived in him, since he lives his life in us. Thus, his perfect sacrifice of praise is expressed and completed in ours, and through Jesus in us, the Father is adequately glorified by us and in us. For by the power and grace of the Eucharist, Jesus grows in us and lives his own life of praise ever more perfectly in us, till at last his perfect sacrifice is completed in all of us, his completed mystical body, the Church.

The Humility of our Amen

A day or two after I wrote this chapter, a young man in our charismatic music ministry told how he had been "chafing at the bit" during a beautiful Eucharistic celebration in which our community had participated. The preaching of the word in that particular celebration had been so moving that the young man had wanted to shout out his joy in unrestrained song and praise. But he complained that the Eucharistic liturgy is so structured that it allows very little leeway for spontaneous praise.

In answer to him, I said that there is a profound reason for a certain amount of restraint in the singing at the Eucharistic celebration. It is not restraint of heartfelt feeling, and not restraint of the beauty and splendor of the singing, but restraint in the sense of not letting our praise eclipse the praise which Jesus himself offers to God in the Eucharistic Prayer. Somehow the liturgy has to give recognition to the fact that in the Eucharist it is primarily the Lord Jesus who is praising the Father through the Eucharistic action.

This recognition is given by the silence of everyone during the Eucharistic Prayer when the priest alone speaks and everyone else listens. At the end of this Prayer the people express their praise in the form of a simple assent to what Jesus has done on their behalf through the ministry of the priest. The assent is given in a brief *Amen!*

The Lord's is the power to offer his sacrifice, ours is only the power to consent that he do it on our behalf. Ours is the power to say yes and to accept, and thus participate in what he does for us. The humble Amen is our Yes to what he alone can do. "No one comes to the Father but by me" (John 14:6).

The Eucharistic Prayer, pronounced only by the priest acting as a minister of Christ, is by its very nature a proclamation. Therefore it is meant to be listened to with silent attention. Our chief intent is to listen with faith and love and acceptance, assenting in our hearts to every element of the proclamation, and then expressing this assent and acceptance aloud in the great Amen at the end. The assent is then to be confirmed by living our lives as an Amen in Christ, by the power and grace given to us in the Eucharistic celebration.

Our lowly Amen at the end of the Eucharistic Prayer may seem very inadequate to our joy, no matter how heartfelt and full of faith the Amen may be. But it really is very adequate, for our very restraint, our silence in the presence of the Lord's own action in the Eucharistic Prayer, is a necessary humility which is itself eloquent praise of Jesus our Savior, and of his God and Father.

Our humble heartfelt assent to Christ's own sacrifice of praise is worth infinitely more than the most eloquent words and songs which might proceed only from ourselves, no matter how much feeling and conviction we might put into them. For by our Amen flowing from a fullness of faith and love, we make the Lord's perfect praise our own.

Therefore whenever we praise God in liturgy or in common prayer, it is well to say, "O Lord, in union with that divine intention with which you carried out praise while on earth, I offer these hours of praise." These are sentiments which were voiced for centuries in the prayer said at the beginning of every liturgical hour in the Divine Office of the Church. Our own praise is worthless if it is not the praise of Jesus continued in us.

The liturgy of the hours and the other forms of community prayer in which we praise God many times a day compensate our eager hearts for the brevity of the Amen to the Eucharistic Prayer, and for the brevity of the other singing in the Eucharistic celebration. The liturgy of the hours has always been carried out as a continuation of the praise begun in the Lord's own praise in the Eucharistic Prayer, and as a preparation for the next Eucharistic celebration. In this same spirit we should carry out all our praising of God. We should realize that our praise is the Lord's own praise of his Father continued and completed in us under the inspiration of his Holy Spirit.

What we have said about restraint in not letting our own expression of praise eclipse the praise which Jesus himself offers in the Eucharist is in no way to be interpreted as discouraging the joy and splendor of singing in the Eucharistic celebration. On the contrary, the joyous realization of what Jesus has done for us in glorifying the Father on the cross gives rise to a desire to praise to the maximum of our ability. This desire should be fulfilled at the times appointed for singing in the Eucharistic celebration and in the best singing of which we are capable.

But there may be times when the Lord's Spirit moves us to eloquent silence in the presence of the Lord, the silent praise which consists in surrendering completely to the interior wonders which he himself is doing in our hearts. Sometimes we are so intent on what he is doing interiorly in our hearts that external praise would be out of place. It would only distract from silent receptivity to his interior presence. This quiet receptivity, inasmuch as it is a deep appreciation of what he is doing in us, is itself magnificent praise.

All truly Christian praise is but the expression of Christ's own Eucharistic praise in our lives and in our words and songs and dances. Our Amen to the Lord's sacrifice of praise, expressed at the end of the Eucharistic Prayer, is only the beginning of an on-going praise in our words and in our works. "Whatever you do, in word or deed, do everything in the name of our Lord Jesus, giving thanks to God the Father through him" (Col. 3:17).

PART FOUR

Christian Life Is Praise

CHAPTER TWENTY-ONE

Alleluia in Light and Color

We usually think of praise only in terms of sound: words and song and joyful music. Perhaps we ought to think of it also in terms of light and color and form, for that is how the natural creation shows forth the glory of God. "The very forms of created things are, as it were, the voices with which they praise their Creator."[43]

The etymology of the word *Alleluia* suggests all this. *Alleluia* is made up of the imperative of *hallel* and of *Ya*, an abbreviated form of Yahweh. The basic meaning of *hallel* is *to be clear*. The word originally referred to clear sound, but more often it was used in reference to color. *Hallel* thus means *to shine forth*. It also means *to celebrate*.

To celebrate something is to cause it to shine forth. In celebrating, we make use of light and color, sound and form, motion and touch, flavor and fragrance. Flowers and music, singing and dancing, eating and drinking, all contribute to the splendor of a celebration.

To praise God is to celebrate him, using every method we can in making him shine forth.

It is true that the word *hallel* as used in the psalms

175

very frequently refers to the use of the voice and music in praising the Lord: "My mouth praises you with joyful lips" (Ps.63:5); "I will praise the name of God with a song" (Ps.69:30). But this vocalization is a response to what is seen and experienced. In words and music we proclaim what we have seen and heard and lived. What we have seen and heard and experienced is God's self-revelation and self-giving. Our praise is our response to God's clarity in revealing himself.

God has revealed himself in his work of creation, but still more vividly in his works of salvation.

"Since the creation of the world," says St. Paul, "invisible realities, God's eternal power and divinity, have become visible, recognized through the things he has made" (Rom.1:20n). There is therefore no excuse for those who obscure God's truth through their perverse lives. "The wrath of God is being revealed from heaven against the irreligious and perverse spirit of men who, in this perversity of theirs, hinder the truth" (Rom.1:18n). To hinder God's truth by wickedness of life is the direct opposite of praising and glorifying him by holiness of life. "Whatever can be known about God is clear to them.... Therefore these men are inexcusable. They certainly had knowledge of God, yet they did not glorify him as God or give him thanks" (Rom.1:19-21n).

But God in his mercy has revealed himself anew, and more marvelously, in his works of salvation, especially in his giving of himself through the grace of his indwelling presence in our hearts. Our only fitting response to the clarity of his merciful self-revelation and self-giving in Jesus is a life lived in love, a life which is praise and thanksgiving.

A life of praise in grateful response to our salvation is

itself a shining forth of God. The perverse lives of sinful men obscure God's glory and hide him from others. The holy lives of the redeemed must manifest him anew. "Let your light so shine before men, that they may see your good works and give glory to your Father who is in heaven" (Matt.5:16).

In these words, as is obvious from their context, Jesus is referring to the good works which are love and justice towards neighbor. For in terms of love, Jesus sums up his description of the good works of righteousness which exceed the righteousness of the scribes and Pharisees: "But I say to you, love your enemies, and pray for those who persecute you, so that you may be sons of your Father who is in heaven; for he makes his sun rise on the evil and on the good, and sends rain on the just and on the unjust" (Matt.5:44-45). We are manifest as true children of God through our works of love, and therefore those who see this love give glory to our Father in heaven. The clarity of God's own love must continue to shine forth in our love for one another.

The Test of Praise: Loving Service

St. Paul, too, puts forth this idea. Just as "our Lord Jesus Christ, ... though he was rich, ... for your sake became poor, so that by his poverty you might become rich" (2 Cor.8:9), so, in continuation of his work of love, we come to the aid of the poor to enrich them. Even though Paul is speaking specifically about alms-giving to the poor, his words are true of all the corporal and spiritual works of mercy. He says that our service of the poor is the test of the validity of our response to the

Gospel, and hence also the test of the value of the praise and glory we give to God:

> This service (of the poor) will prove to them what you are, and they will give glory to God for your obedience in professing the Gospel of Christ, and for your generosity in sharing with them and with all. (2 Cor.9:12-13*b*)

Another translation puts it this way:

> Under the test of this service, you will glorify God by your obedience in acknowledging the Gospel of Christ. . . . (9:13*r*)

Thus, St. Augustine's famous definition of glory is verified above all where God is manifested in man's love. Augustine says, "Glory is being clearly known with praise" (*clara cum laude notitia*). This definition takes into account both God's clarity shining forth, and our response to this by praising him. Glory is not simply God's self-manifestation, but is also our receiving of this manifestation in clear knowledge, and our loving response in praise. We see God's love manifest in our brother's love for us, and we praise our Father in heaven.

Love is the Fullness of Praise

The essence of praise, according to Augustine, is love. Addressing his Creator, Augustine says: "Let your works praise you that we may love you, and let us love you that your works may praise you."[43] The works of God praise him through the love of God which they evoke in us. The praise of God by his works is completed only when we respond to their message by loving the God they manifest. This love is the perfect praise.

And because love in us is God's most perfect work, it in turn evokes praise in still other people. And the joy of this love spontaneously bursts forth in celebration, in song and dance and all the rest. Chief among God's works are his holy people and the love which he himself inspires in them by his Holy Spirit. Thus God's salvation work shines forth in our works of love for our fellowmen and his clarity is manifest. That is why our works of love evoke love of God and praise of him. "Let your light so shine before men that they may see your good works and give glory to your Father who is in heaven" (Matt.5:16).

Christian *hallel* is therefore a shining forth of God in our lives, and evokes a *hallel* of celebration in song and music and community praise: Alleluia! Christian liturgy is a celebration of his joy which God has fashioned in us by pouring out his own love into our hearts and into our lives.

Commenting on the words of the psalm, "Sing to the Lord a new song," Augustine says, "Let our life, not our tongue, chant this new song" (On Ps.32). According to Augustine, as we have seen, the life that experiences jubilation, and therefore sings, is the life that experiences God in love. All external Christian praise and celebration is the expression of love's joy in the Lord.

Dispelling the Obscurity

Our works of love, then, far more than all the beauties

179

of nature, evoke love and praise of God. This is an exceedingly important truth for our times when God's glory has been so obscured by the perversity of human life. It has been obscured especially by man's selfishness in abusing nature. We are not speaking merely of the abuse of ecology, but of something more radical which is truly criminal: the widespread use of God's creation for purposes of greed, involving the exploitation not simply of natural wealth but the manipulation and exploitation of human persons. God's love and glory are so hidden by the selfish way in which modern economy and political and social life are organized that the victims of this abuse of God's love are tempted to cry out, "There is no God!" God's love is obscured by man's selfishness, which has led to untold violence and hatred and war in every quarter of the globe.

Only when man's work and science and technology and art once again express love and justice can God again clearly shine forth in the world of men. In love, all of us must serve not only the poor, but one another. All our work and business and secular affairs must be a service to our fellowmen rendered in love. Only then will God be glorified in all that we do. Only then will our work be praise, in response to God's love which shines forth in the whole of the material creation. Then will our fellowmen see the love in our works, and will come to know the loving Father whose love has been poured out into our hearts by the Holy Spirit.

We could expand upon Augustine's words, "Let your works praise you that we may love you, and let us love you that your works may praise you." We could put it this way: "Let your work of creation praise you through the love in which we use this creation, glorifying you by using all this love for our fellowmen, whom we see as your children and our brothers."

The Alleluia in Work

In St. Jerome's day, the plowmen of Bethlehem and the fishermen of Galilee sang "Alleluia" as they worked. And we have seen the jubilation of the harvesters and vintagers in Italy and North Africa in St. Augustine's times. Joy like this was experienced in work in biblical times, too. Several Hebrew words for "praise" have their origin, it seems, in the joy of human work. For example, *hillool* is a word for praise which had its origin in harvest joy. The word is derived from *hallel*, and means "a *celebration* in thanksgiving for the harvest." The very offering of the fruits of the harvest was a *hillool*, a praise to God: "In the fourth year all the fruit of the trees shall be holy, to *praise* the Lord (*hillool*)" (Lev.19:24).

Another example may be *zamar*, which means both "to trim a vine" and "to touch the strings of a musical instrument, to play upon it, to make music accompanied by the voice; hence, to celebrate in song and music, to sing forth praises."

Our contemporary inability to experience "harvest joy" like this in our work is due in part to our loss of healthy human relationships in our daily work-life. The joy of life is lost in our impersonal, dehumanizing, technological society. Hence we need to learn again how to celebrate. Once again we need the Alleluias of the craftsman, the merchant, the laborer. When people learn again to serve their fellowmen in love by their work, love's joy in their hearts will again burst forth in songs of celebration of God's goodness. Amen! Alleluia!

181

For these reasons we should take seriously the words of Hebrews: "We must consider how to rouse each other to love and good deeds. We should not absent ourselves from the assembly, as some do, but encourage one another" (Heb.10:24-25n). Rouse one another in love and to love in community prayer! Do not stay away from the sacred liturgy, which is the celebration of God's love and of ours. Come together to seek out the God who rejoices in the whole of his creation, but above all in his children. Come together to seek out these children of God to rejoice with them. Take your fellowmen with you, inviting them with words like those used in Israel of old: "Come, let us sing joyfully to the Lord; let us acclaim the Rock of our salvation. Let us greet him with thanksgiving; let us joyfully sing psalms to him" (Ps.95:1-2n).

The charismatic renewal has spread in such a phenomenal way precisely because once again the God of love is shining forth in the splendor of people's love for one another as they gather together to praise the Lord. Everything that happens at the prayer meeting is *hallel*: the clear shining forth of the Lord, in word and song and other colorful elements of celebration, but especially in the form and light and splendor of true Christian love.

Sincere community praise, where God's clarity shines forth in splendid celebration, causes the participants to go forth with an Alleluia in their heart and on their lips. And their daily lives become an Alleluia in light and color as God shines forth in their work of love. "In everything you do, act without grumbling or arguing; prove yourselves innocent and straightforward, children of God beyond reproach in the midst of a perverse and depraved generation—among whom you shine like stars in the sky while holding fast to the word of life" (Phil. 2:14-16n).

CHAPTER TWENTY-TWO

The Christian Life:
A Sacrifice of Praise

St. Paul describes the whole Christian life as a eucharist, a sacrifice of praise and thanksgiving offered in gratitude to the divine love and mercy. "Whatever you do, in word or deed, do everything in the name of the Lord Jesus, giving thanks to God the Father through him" (Col. 3:17).

Paul is always emphatic in insisting on the complete gratuitousness of God's love for men. Mankind in no way deserves to be loved by God, for all of us come into this world as enemies of God. "We were by nature children of wrath" (Eph.2:3). "All have sinned and fall short of the glory of God" (Rom.3:23). However, precisely because the decadence of man is total and incurable, God intervenes, in the work of redemption, to show his glory, to show his own true nature which is all goodness and loving kindness. "Where sin increased," says Paul, "grace has abounded all the more" (Rom.5:20).

Grace, in Paul's vocabulary, is first of all something in God himself. It is God's gracious love for us; it is God himself loving and giving himself in infinite mercy and generosity, loving entirely gratuitously, loving us who in no way deserve his love. God loves us not because we are loveable, but sheerly because he is love. "Not that we loved God but that he loved us and sent his Son to be the expiation for our sins" (1 John 4:10).

Speaking of this gracious, gratuitous love, Paul says,

> But God, who is rich in mercy, out of the great love with which he loved us, even when we were dead through our trespasses, made us alive together with Christ (by grace you have been saved), and raised us up with him, and made us sit with him in the heavenly places in Christ Jesus, that in the coming ages he might show the immeasurable riches of his grace in kindness toward us in Christ Jesus. For by grace you have been saved through faith; and this is not your own doing, it is the gift of God. (Eph.2:4-8)

Since divine love is always creative, it produces something in us, namely, sanctifying grace, a sheer gift of God which is in no way deserved, which makes us children of God pleasing to Him. "Where sin increased, grace has abounded all the more" (Rom.5:20). The superabounding merciful love of God overflowed with gifts of grace which swallowed up and destroyed sin and death. To say that God gives his grace is to say that he prodigally pours forth his love, his mercy, his loving kindness. Gratuitousness is the essential mark of the divine love for us.

Jesus himself is the supreme grace of God to us, in whose Person all grace is given. "He who did not spare his own Son but gave him up for us all, will he not also

185

give us all things with him?" (Rom.8:32). The Son gave up his human life on the cross, that God might give his divine life to us by grace. In Christ, God gives us all things, because he gives himself to us in Christ.

And to whom does he give himself so graciously? To us who were sinners. "God shows his love for us in that while we were yet sinners Christ died for us" (Rom.5:8). The shedding of Christ's precious blood for us sinners accentuates to us the merciful gratuitousness of divine generosity. To prove that he wills to give us all things— himself in eternal life, and all that we need on the way—God gave his Son, and the Son gave his life, shedding his blood for us.

Praise: The Response To Grace

What return can man make for this initiative of divine love? Paul gives the answer in the second part of his letter to the Romans. If the first part of his letter is a description of God's mercy, the second half describes our only fitting response to this mercy.

The first eleven chapters of Romans are a magnificent description of the merciful love which has rescued both Jew and Gentile from the disobedience of sin. "For God has consigned all men to disobedience, that he may have mercy upon all" (Rom.11:32). Thus summing up all that he has said thus far to the Romans, Paul then bursts into a marvelous hymn extolling the magnificence of the divine mercy:

> O the depth of the riches and wisdom and knowledge of God! How unsearchable are his judgments

and how inscrutable his ways! For who has known the mind of the Lord, or who has been his counselor? Or who has given a gift to him that he might be repaid? For from him and through him and to him are all things. To him be glory for ever. Amen. (Rom.11:33-36)

After his hymn extolling God's mercy, Paul calls for a response to this mercy: "I appeal to you therefore, brethren, by the mercies of God, to present your bodies as a living sacrifice, holy and acceptable to God, which is your spiritual worship" (Rom.12:1). "Body," in Paul's vocabulary, means the whole living person. Our return to God's mercy is the living of our whole life as a sacrifice of praise and thanksgiving.

Paul goes on to spell out in detail how this is to be done. He calls for the practice of all the virtues which express Christian community love, all the virtues necessary for building up the Body of Christ: humility, patience, hospitality, brotherly affection, and so on (Rom.12:3-21). This love for our fellowmen is to be lived as an expression of our thanksgiving to God, as our sacrifice of praise of his love, as our living eucharist.

Such is the logical response we owe to the divine graciousness and merciful love—to love one another as he has loved us, and thus offer our whole being in praise and thanksgiving as "a living sacrifice" (Rom.12:1). "A living sacrifice of praise," says Eucharistic Prayer IV.

Paul repeats the same message in his letter to the Ephesians. We are to imitate the divine love and generosity which is manifest in Christ's consecration of himself on the cross as a sacrifice for our salvation. "Therefore be imitators of God, as beloved children. And walk

187

in love, as Christ loved us and gave himself up for us, a fragrant offering and sacrifice to God" (Eph.5:1-2).

The method and manner of offering ourselves as such a sacrifice of praise and grateful love is precisely prescribed: "Walk in love, do the works of love." Paul has just finished a long list of the works of love which build up the mystical body of Christ, and now summarizes them by showing that all this is our way of delivering ourselves to God in gratitude and praise, in love like Christ's. Love for one another is the only fitting return to God's love for us. "Be kind to one another, tenderhearted, forgiving one another, as God in Christ forgave you" (Eph.4:32). "Therefore, putting away falsehood, let every one speak the truth with his neighbor, for we are members of one another" (Eph.4:25). "Do not let the sun go down on your anger.... Let the thief no longer steal, but rather let him labor, doing honest work with his hands, so that he may be able to give to those in need" (Eph.4:26-28). And so on.

The need of such an offering to God through effective brotherly love imposes itself inescapably once we become aware of the entirely gratuitous gift of salvation from God's merciful love. The only fitting way to live henceforth is to offer oneself, soul and body, as a living sacrifice of praise, "to the praise of his glorious grace which he freely bestowed on us in the Beloved" (Eph.1:6). God's gracious generosity toward us inspires in us the magnificent motivation of our whole Christian life: in utter generosity toward one another, we spend ourselves and are spent as a living eucharist. "Do this in memory of me" (Luke 22:19).

St. Paul himself is forever giving thanks, and is repeatedly exhorting his readers to do likewise. In analysing the large number of texts in which he speaks of thanksgiving, we see that for him praise and thanksgiving to God is not just one among many interior sentiments, nor even a high form of prayer. The giving of thanks is the permanent dynamic attitude of a sinful creature mercifully saved, who knows he is the object of infinite love, who depends upon this love, who accepts it gratefully, and sings of it. Joyous hymns of gratitude should be ever bursting from the Christian heart. "Be thankful.... Sing psalms and hymns and spiritual songs with thankfulness in your hearts to God. And whatever you do, in word or deed, do everything in the name of the Lord Jesus, giving thanks to God the Father through him" (Col.3:15-17; cf.,Eph.5:19-20).

Paul has still more wonderful things to say about love's response to divine love. Once we fully appreciate the infinite greatness of God's loving kindness towards us, we give ourselves over so totally to him in a return of love that nothing can separate us from his love. Our love is so welded to the divine love in one mutual love that no trials, no sufferings, no persecutions can separate us from God's love given to us in Christ:

> If God is for us, who is against us? He who did not spare his own Son but gave him up for us all, will he not also give us all things with him? ... Who shall separate us from the love of Christ? Shall tribulation, or distress, or persecution, or famine, or nakedness, or peril, or sword? As it is written, "For your sake we are being killed all the day long; we are regarded as sheep to be slaughtered." No, in all these things we are more than conquerors through him who loved us. For I am sure that neither death,

nor life, nor angels, nor principalities, nor things present, nor things to come, nor powers, nor height, nor depth, nor anything else in all creation, will be able to separate us from the love of God in Christ Jesus our Lord. (Rom.8:31-39)

Such is our sacrifice of praise to God in grateful love. We endure all things for him, who suffered all things for us. Our whole life becomes *laus gloriae*: "the praise of his glory" (Eph.1:12,14), "the praise of his glorious grace which he bestowed on us in the Beloved" (Eph.1:6).

The Witness of Elizabeth of the Trinity

"It is my dream to be 'the Praise of His Glory' "
These are the words written by Elizabeth of the Trinity, a French Carmelite nun, at the head of the notes she made during her last retreat, shortly before her death in 1906. She was convinced that "Praise of his Glory" (Eph.1:12), was her true God-given name, the name expressing her eternal vocation. But she knew that her whole being could be praise of his glory only if she died completely to self in Jesus, who died to self and accepted his cross, saying, "Father, glorify your name!" (John 12:28).

We summarize some of Elizabeth's own words from that retreat:

The song of a Praise of Glory on the first day of her retreat should be: 'I know nothing, I desire to know nothing but Christ, and the fellowship of his sufferings, being made conformable to his death (Phil.3:10), conformable to the image of his Son (Rom.8:29), who was crucified by love.' Only when I become completely identified with my crucified Lord, dwelling wholly in him and he in me, shall I fulfill my eternal vocation for which God chose me in him in the beginning, and which I shall fulfill in eternity, when, immersed in the bosom of the Trinity, I shall be the unceasing 'Praise of his Glory."[44]

CHAPTER TWENTY-THREE

How a Family Praises God

In the days when this book was being written, a woman came to me for spiritual guidance, and told me a remarkable story about God's working in her family.

For some years the woman had been suffering from an infirmity which left her ever more crippled. As she became more and more helpless, she was faced with this worry: If I conceive another child, will I be able to care for it? Will I be able to fulfill my maternal responsibilities?

Then one night she received a clear call from God, who offered pregnancy to her if she was willing to welcome it. She told her husband this, and he agreed that they should welcome the child, and trust the Lord to take care of his own. The mother knew that very night that she had conceived.

Once the child came there was an astonishing remission of the woman's infirmity, so that she was able to care for the child perfectly, though that was about all she could do. Since she could do little else, she spent long hours with the child, in wonderful communion with her. She experienced a presence of God in the child. God was loving her in the child. God was giving her love through the child's response to her love.

She experienced all of this as something done in her by God in sheer love. She was very conscious of her personal unworthiness and of her sinfulness, yet the Lord chose to reveal a divine mystery in her. She had a living experience of a specific facet of the mystery of Christ, of how God lives in his people and loves in them. She experienced her own love for the child as God's love for the child, just as she experienced the child's love for her as God's love for her.

When she spoke of this mystery with her husband, he did not fully understand at first what was happening. He suggested that all of this was only the result of her own possessive love of the child, a love which was focusing too exclusively on this one infant and neglecting her other children. But she examined her conscience carefully on this matter, and prayed earnestly for enlightenment. The answer to her prayer came in the form of the same experience of divine love for her other children and for her husband.

This woman vividly experienced what the rest of us usually know only in the darkness of faith: that God indeed does love through our Christian love. This is the hidden, deeper nature of all authentic Christian love.

This infant was always filled with an extraordinary peace and joy and eager response to everything. The mother saw the child as a magnificent praise of God, an eloquent expression of the Scriptural truth: "Out of the mouths of babes and sucklings you have brought perfect praise" (Matt.21:16; cf.,Ps.8:2). The whole being of the child was praise and joy. Observing her, the mother realized as never before that all of us are created for joy in the Lord.

193

For weeks, that was the woman's constant meditation. Then one morning she phoned me to tell me how a family praises God, for I had asked her to tell me what praise meant in her children's lives. The following are her words, which I took down as well as I could as she spoke them on the phone.

The true praise of God is living life to the full, enjoying it thoroughly, in the Christian way. The whole being of my joyful child seems to be saying that. One best praises God by being what God meant one to be.

I have been meditating on the Holy Family of Jesus, Mary and Joseph. How did Jesus praise the Father? By doing what the Father told him to do, by being what the Father wanted him to be. He praised God by his life of obedience. And Joseph praised God by being a carpenter, living his daily life to the full. Mary praised God by being mother and wife, doing what God intended for her.

A true marriage is praise to God, for it is a love lived together, a life lived in witness, when lived as God intended that it should be lived. A baby praises God, not verbally, but with its whole being, by its utter delight in life, by being what it is supposed to be. What happens as a child grows? Why does not this joy continue?

A child will continue in joy and praise of God if it lives in an environment of praise and joy. Its joy will continue if it lives its whole life as a process of growth towards God's eternal life, if its whole life is ever in the process of the new life given in baptism, if God's life in it is ever growing. If a family is truly

*a community in God, a cell in the body of Christ, if
it is the kind of family God intended it to be,
characterized by God's own creative love, then it
will be a family of joy and praise.*

*In such a family circle, praise is "contagious." At
the breakfast table our family has morning prayer
and our little girl raises her hands in prayer and
claps her hands for joy in imitation of her praying
parents and brothers and sisters. This in turn
inspires the older children to praise God more fer-
vently.*

Praise Springs from Baptismal Grace

The mother whose witness we have just heard expressed an important principle to be remembered in
drawing out the best that is in a child. God's own life is
already in the child because of baptism, and its whole
life will be a process of steady growth towards eternal
life in God, if we provide for it a family and community
environment which also is life in God, life in the body of
Christ. Praise and worship of God is already rooted in
the child's heart from the instant of baptism, for from
that moment Christ dwells in that heart, and his Holy
Spirit is in that heart to form in it Christ's own relationship with the Father in love and praise.

Another mother gave these reflections on praise in her
home:

*Instead of us trying to teach the children to praise,
we should be watching them so we learn how to
praise God perfectly. A baby gives perfect praise*

195

because he is totally himself, totally accepting the way he is. A young child usually accepts the conditions into which he is born. He is not concerned with where he lives or what he eats, not concerned with comparing himself with others, not concerned with the appearance of things. He is totally satisfied if he is loved and accepted. As long as we meet his basic needs, he delights in being himself. He delights in his food, his burp, his bath, the smiles he receives, his hands, his feet, his voice. He truly praises God for himself as a unique creation. We should not really desire to remain children, but to remain childlike.

Nature is a perfect praise to God when not interfered with. It grows exactly as God ordained it to grow. Trees grow up, not down, produce fruits at the proper time, and not before. We praise God most when we are fully ourselves, fully human with the development of all our senses, our mind and heart, our bodies. By becoming more myself, developing my gifts and potentialities, I praise God more perfectly. As a person accepts himself and those around him, he truly praises God.

A baby is totally dependent on its parents for everything. He does nothing for the parents in a physical way, yet they truly delight in him, delight in him just because he exists. We need this same attitude towards God—one of total dependence. Our real problem is that we are strong but not strong enough, weak but not weak enough. We need to be totally dependent on God. It is through this humble experience as a child that God can raise us up.

CHAPTER TWENTY-FOUR

The Yes to Life

My Amen to the preaching of God's word is a Yes to what God wills to do in my life, and therefore it is a Yes to life. It is a Yes to Jesus, the Lord of every life, who by his power and Spirit at work in me wills to give fullness of meaning and value to my life. My Yes lets Jesus be Lord, Lord of every event and detail in my life, so that he might transform my whole life and my total being into an Alleluia of perfect praise to God.

To say Yes to the Lord and to his work in my life is to say Yes also to all the materials with which he works—my life as he finds it, with all its sinfulness as well as with its good points, with its sicknesses and sufferings as well as with its strengths and talents.

To say Yes to the Lord is to say Yes to what he wants to make of these materials. For his purposes to be accomplished, I have to say Yes to every situation in which I find myself, no matter how miserable it may be, whether this misery stems from my own sinfulness, or from the sinfulness of those about me, or from the sinfulness of those who went before me. I have to accept myself as I am and where I am. I have to accept my situation as it is, praising the Lord who is Lord of all of this, Lord of every detail in my life, working in all things for my good through my Yes to him. For it is through my praise of the Lord, this Amen to his loving power and presence in every situation, that he works for my good.

To praise him in every imaginable situation, even the most miserable, is to accept the truth of the Gospel as summed up by St. Paul: "We know that in everything God works for good with those who love him, who are called according to his purpose" (Rom.8:28). The next verse tells us what this purpose is: "to (conform us) to the image of his Son, in order that he might be the first-born among many brethren" (Rom.8:29).

These words are truly a beautiful summary of the Gospel. For the good news is this: in everything, even in our sinfulness, God our Savior is at work by his redeeming power, bringing forth our good through our Yes to him. "Those who love him" (Rom.8:28), are those who say Yes to him in the Holy Spirit of adoption, crying "Abba, Father" (Rom.8:15). Through this Yes, his purpose of conforming us to the image of his Son is accomplished. For Jesus was all Yes! His Yes was his loving response to his Father's loving purposes. Through my conformity with Jesus in his Yes, he brings me through sufferings and death to the fullness of life in him.

My Yes to the Lord Jesus and to his redeeming work in me cancels out the No of sin and all its miserable effects. But if I continue to say no to Jesus, I not only remain in my sin, I compound that sin, and I deepen its misery in my own life and in those of my fellowmen.

There are many ways of saying No to him. I say No

to the Lord by saying No to the providential circumstances of my life, resenting my situation, feeling sorry for myself, indulging in self-pity, and blaming everyone and anyone for my misery. I say No to him be refusing to accept my life as it is and myself as I am and failing to offer all this to the Lord's redeeming presence and transforming power. But I say Yes to him, I open myself to his presence and power, by praising him in every situation, acknowledging him as my Lord and Lord of this situation.

My Amen to the good news of his power working in me is never without an Alleluia of joyous praise, for this good news tells about truly magnificent wonders that he wills to accomplish in me. Whatever my circumstances, I say "Amen (So be it)! Alleluia (Praise the Lord)!" I accept the situation and the Lord's presence and wonderful purpose in that situation. Inevitably my Amen will be followed by a glorious Alleluia of praise and thanksgiving for the marvels he has been able to accomplish in me because I have said Yes!

Amen! Alleluia!

A remarkable witness to this is the spirituality of the Sisters of Jesus Crucified, a congregation of religious women who are physically handicapped: blind, deaf, crippled, chronically sick.[45] Their whole spirituality is summed up in their motto: *Amen! Alleluia!*. Their Amen of acceptance of their condition is not a grudging resignation. It is a joyous *Yes* to the loving providence of their Lord, a whole-hearted *Praise the Lord* to him who works in all things for the good of those who love him.

199

Self-pity, self-centered feeling sorry for themselves because of their handicaps, is totally ruled out of their lives by their *Amen! Alleluia!* Their whole attention is focused on the Lord, not on their sicknesses and handicaps. Theirs is a vocation to joyous acceptance of the Lord, who works out his own redeeming purposes in their hardships. "This illness is not unto death; it is for the glory of God, so that the Son of God may be glorified by means of it" (John 11:4).

Dispelling Crippling Resentments

In life's troubles, all of us have a tendency to bewail our fate and to waste our vitality and energies on resentment, on feeling sorry for ourselves, and on blaming others for our difficult situations. Sometimes we even go so far as to be angry with God. But in doing all of this, we sink only more deeply into the swamp of our misery. Resenting others and blaming them, even if their sins are responsible for our difficulties, is not the solution to our problems. The decisive factor in every difficult situation in our life is our own right response to it, our Yes to God's loving providence which works for good with those who love him.

Blaming others only compounds our misery. Adam blamed Eve for his sin, instead of being man enough to accept his own responsibility for his fall. Eve in turn blamed Satan, instead of being woman enough to admit her own guilt in the matter. Satan had deceived the two by suggesting to them that God was unfair to them in trying to keep them from knowledge. Thus the deceiver was instigating anger against God.

It is true that we lead one another into sin, as Eve tempted Adam and as Satan tempted Eve. But God tempts no one; and ultimately, no matter who or which creature tempts us, each one of us is responsible for his own sins, or for his refusal to sin:

> Let no one say when he is tempted, "I am tempted by God"; for God cannot be tempted with evil and he himself tempts no one; but each person is tempted when he is lured and enticed by his own desire. Then desire when it has conceived gives birth to sin; and sin when it is full-grown brings forth death. (James 1:13-15)

Others tempt us only because they appeal to our own inner desire, and it is within our power to say Yes or No in every situation. Thus the decisive factor in every situation in our life is our personal response to it. Whatever unfortunate experiences come to us in life from the conduct of others, or from any causes whatsoever, the ultimate outcome for good or for evil for us depends upon our personal response. The response, of course, is made only with the help of God's grace. Each one remains, whatever be the influences affecting him, the principal agent of his own success or failure in life. Resenting others and casting blame upon them, even when they are guilty, only heightens our troubles and makes them more complex and more ensnaring.

No matter whose fault made my life situation the way it is—whether my own sins or the sins of my parents, the sins of my contemporaries or the sins of my ancestors— the way out is always open to me. The open door is my Yes to the redeeming presence of the Lord, who in all things works with those who love him, for their good.

Therefore instead of wasting my life and my vitality on resentment of others and of my situation, my Yes to the redeeming Lord will free me. To praise him in every situation, no matter how miserable it may be, is to accept his redeeming presence and power and to transform my trial into joy. To praise the Lord in my troubles is to open my heart to the peace and joy which dispels all anger and resentment, all despair and discouragement.

The Lord's will to save and sanctify us is operative in our Yes to him in whatever conditions we find ourselves. The Lord Jesus is always there where we are, and our praise of him and acceptance of him as Lord in every situation is perfect only through our Yes to things as they are. We dispel our resentments through knowing in faith that he has everything under control and is working all things out to our good through our *Amen! Alleluia!*, our Yes of praise of him. To say Yes to the Lord is to say Yes to life.

The On-Going Yes

My Yes must continue throughout the situation as God continues to work in the situation for my good. My Yes is the gift of his grace, and at the same time it is truly *my* Yes. "Work out your own salvation with fear and trembling; for God is at work in you, both to will and to work for his good pleasure" (Phil.2:12-13). My good will, my Yes to the Lord, is the work of his grace in my heart. My continuing Yes, that is, my work of cooperation with his good purposes, is also the work of his grace in my heart. But it is truly my work, too, in which his grace works.

God truly helps those who help themselves, for his saving and healing work in our lives is brought to completion only through our working with him in response to his grace. For example, he will heal me completely of my sinful habits only through my own work of self-discipline. The fullness of his grace comes to me only in and through my own works of cooperation with him. I hinder the full fruitfulness of his grace if I fail to help myself by working with him, performing the good actions he expects of me, the acts of self-control, patience, kindness, goodness, faithfulness, purity, gentleness, love, joy, and peace, and all the other "fruits of the Spirit" (cf.,Gal.5:22-23). The fruits of the Spirit are the works of virtue which the Lord Jesus ripens in us through our own working with him (Phil.1:11). "For God is at work in you, both to will and to work for his good pleasure" (Phil.2:13).

My continuing Yes is my on-going carrying out of the works which God works in me through the Yes which is my cooperation. Christian life is an on-going combat against evil; a continuing struggle to embrace God. A later chapter contains the witness of my friends concerning this spiritual warfare.

CHAPTER TWENTY-FIVE

Discouragement Is "No" to the Lord

Another way of saying No to the Lord and to life is through self-condemnation. In this case I do not blame God or Satan or my fellowmen for my misery; I blame myself, in a sinful bitter remorse over my sins. I linger over my sins as though my sinful condition were hopeless, instead of accepting the Lord's loving forgiveness, and praising him as my redeeming Lord.

This was not how St. Peter acted. Peter did indeed weep bitterly over his sin of denying the Lord (Luke 22:62). But his tears were a response to the Lord's look at him (Luke 22:61), and therefore they were more a response to love than an expression of disappointment with self. They were tears of loving repentance rather than tears of bitter, self-condemning remorse.

Self-condemnation usually springs from one's hurt pride, rather than from love of the one we have offended. Our pride is hurt because we have fallen, and we are bitterly disappointed with self. We indulge in discouragement and self-condemnation. We are not humble enough to accept our condition as sinner, and we do not entrust our sinfulness to the Lord's merciful presence and forgiveness. Instead of praising the Lord's redeeming love by accepting it in humility, we remain in our discouragement and disappointment with self.

Peter did not act in this way. Unlike Judas, who condemned himself and hanged himself in despair over his sin (Matt.27:5), Peter did not condemn himself. Rather, in humility he admitted his sinfulness and accepted the Lord's merciful love and forgiveness. When he saw Jesus again after the Resurrection, he could humbly admit that once again, by the Lord's gift, he loved the Lord: "You know that I love you" (John 21:15).

The Lord on this occasion drew from Peter's heart the right mixture of true sorrow for his sin and joyful acceptance of forgiveness. He had the air of doubting that Peter loved him; three times he asked, "Do you love me?" (John 21:15-17). Peter was grieved by this seeming doubt: Lord, you know everything, you know that I love you, and still you make me say it three times!

But Jesus knew what he was about. He was showing Peter, and us, that the love and forgiveness which we accept from him must not be taken for granted and inadequately appreciated. We must deeply recognize our sinfulness if we are to deeply appreciate his loving mercy. The Lord asked three times, "Do you love me?" to remind Peter that three times he had denied him. Repentance for the triple sin must be confessed in a triple act of love.

My praise of the Lord's mercy must spring from a consciousness of the sinfulness which was healed by that mercy, "I will sing of the mercies of the Lord forever!"

(Ps.89:1*k*). "I will celebrate your love forever, Yahweh!" (Ps.89:1*j*). My joyous praise of his mercy must stem from a continuing consciousness that of myself I am still a sinner, still capable of falling. His steadfast love is forever a merciful love, for of myself, without his love, I would be forever a sinner.

Paul's Praise of God's Mercy

St. Paul, like St. Peter, never fell into despairing self-condemnation. He who had persecuted the Lord writes, "There is therefore now no condemnation for those who are in Christ Jesus" (Rom.8:1). Paul's whole life and continuing prayer is a hymn of acceptance of God's mercy: "to the praise of his glorious grace which he freely bestowed on us in the Beloved. In him we have redemption through his blood, the forgiveness of our trespasses" (Eph.1:6-7).

Paul's desire to make his whole life a hymn of praise springs from his personal experience of mercy: "Though I formerly blasphemed and persecuted and insulted him, ... I received mercy because I had acted ignorantly in unbelief. ... I am the foremost of sinners; but I received mercy for this reason, that in me, as the foremost, Jesus Christ might display his perfect patience for an example to those who were to believe in him for eternal life. To the King of ages, immortal, invisible, the only God, be honor and glory for ever and ever. Amen." (1 Tim. 1:13-17).

For all his joyous praise of God's merciful forgiveness, we detect in Paul a trace of regret and continuing sorrow over his past sinfulness: "I am the least of the apostles

... because I persecuted the church of God." But he adds at once, "But by the grace of God I am what I am, and his grace toward me was not in vain" (1 Cor. 15:9-10). He too, like Peter, accepts the Lord's love, and praises his grace. His regret and sorrow over his sinfulness is not self-condemning remorse, but is rather loving contrition. Such contrition continues along with a repentant sinner's joy over God's merciful forgiveness. For the redeemed never forget that of themselves they are sinners, and they sing the Lord's mercies forever.

Augustine's Joyous Contrition

Augustine, too, like Peter and Paul, never forgot that he was a sinner, and was ever receiving God's mercy. Though his *Confessions* are primarily a confession of God's merciful love, they are such precisely because they are also a confession of his own sinfulness. "I confess with inward exultation yet trembling, with inward sorrow yet with hope as well."[46]

Augustine's inward exultation in God's merciful love and forgiveness is forever seasoned with humility and with the healthy fear of his own capacity for sin: the "fear and trembling" with which we work out our salvation (Phil.2:13). His "inward sorrow with hope" is not self-condemning, despairing remorse, but the humble trust in God's merciful love which characterizes all true Christian sorrow for sin. This sorrow is not the worldly sorrow which produces death (2 Cor.7:10), but the sorrow according to God which "produces a repentance that leads to salvation, and brings no regret" (2 Cor.7:9). The sorrow according to God produces repentance, that is, the fruits of repentance, of which we have spoken. The sorrow which produces death is the self-centered remorse which is too proud to accept forgiveness.

Augustine had momentarily tended in this direction, and was tempted to run away: "terrified by my sins and the mass of my misery, I had pondered in my heart and thought of flight into the desert, but You forbade me and strengthened me, saying, 'Christ died for all, that they also who live may now not live to themselves, but with him who died for them.'"[47] God would not let Augustine hide himself in bitter remorse, but called him into the community of those who share in the blood of their redemption. "He, your Only One, has redeemed me with his blood. . . . I think upon the price of my redemption, I eat it and drink it and give it to others to eat and drink. Being poor, I desire to be filled with it among those who eat and are filled (Ps.22:27): 'and they shall praise the Lord that seek him.'"[48]

Jubilation, Fruit of Contrition

Peter and Paul and Augustine all experienced the jubilation which is the fruit of loving contrition for sin. Remorse and self-condemnation lead only to bitterness and death. But contrition and the acceptance of God's redeeming love lead to peace and joy. Repentance is returning home to the Father's house. The joyful noise of dancing resounds through the countryside because a lost son has found his way home, a dead man has come alive (Luke 15:25,32). The return home is a resurrection from the dead, and calls for joyous celebration. "We had to celebrate and rejoice! This brother of yours was dead, and has come back to life. He was lost, and is found" (Luke 15:32n).

"Say Yes To The Weakness!"

A few days after this chapter was written, I received a letter from a cloistered nun who had been experiencing profoundly the very realities of which I have written. She had not seen what I wrote, yet she described the realities in a remarkably similar way. But her words are far more convincing than mine, because she is describing what she has lived. For months she had been suffering over the human frailities of the nuns in her community, over their seeming spiritual blindness and their lack of profound holiness. But her fretting over the weakness of the others was rooted in her pride, which had not yet detected or admitted her personal fraility. Then during her retreat—the very days I was writing this chapter—the Lord spoke to her about these matters. Here is her report to me about what he asked of her. (By this time she had become deeply aware of her own pride and weakness):

> *With intense insistence he seemed to be telling me: "Say Yes to the weakness!" I did, and all that day I pondered what it meant. It means more than accept the weakness. But it certainly does not mean to assent to what is sin and refusal of God's love. It means the Yes of dependence, of wanting to be without defense or resistance before him, of exposing all my weakness and sinfulness to his purifying fire, glad to bring it to him who came for*

those who need a physician. I must say Yes to my weakness precisely in this human situation, to my inability to cope with it, my helplessness to change or improve it. I must say Yes to the weakness of each one whom I love and for whom I am concerned, and Yes to our corporate community weakness.

In the whole mystery of incarnation, Jesus was limited by the weakness of sinful flesh on every side. Even in his own flesh he took on these limitations. "He who acknowledges that Jesus has come in the flesh is of God" (1 John 4:2).

At this point in her letter, I add these reflections of my own: Jesus said Yes to the weakness of flesh by assuming it in his own person and living among us who are flesh. That is an essential of Christian faith. "Every spirit which confesses that Jesus Christ has come in the flesh is of God" (1 John 4:2). In Jesus and with him we must say Yes to the helplessness of our human conditions as flesh, exposing it all to the redeeming power of the risen Lord, who broke out of the flesh into the glory of the resurrection.

Sister's letter continues:

Our Lord could not really penetrate freely into other hearts till he passed through death and broke the bonds of flesh in his risen body. I must say Yes to Jesus who comes in my flesh, too, who hides his glorious power in this vessel of clay, and is limited by it, in a sense. Once again I come back to "gladly will I glory in my infirmities" (2 Cor.12:9), for if I find favor in his sight, it is because of my need, the weakness in which his power may be made perfect.

210

Through my Yes to my weakness (and to the weakness of all my fellowmen) God is praised and glorified, for by my Yes I accept his saving help. Through my humble admission of my neediness and my yielding of my helplessness to him, the glory of his loving and redeeming power breaks into my life and becomes operative and manifest. "We have this treasure in earthen vessels, to show that the transcendent power belongs to God and not to us. We are ... always carrying in the body the death of Jesus, so that the life of Jesus may also be manifested in our bodies" (2 Cor.4:7,10).

As long as I resist his glorious life and power by my proud self-sufficiency and refusal to accept my helplessness, I am deprived of the joy of the Lord which can be poured only into the poor in spirit, the humble and contrite of heart.

Jubilation and the Gift of Tears

A Dallas business man, who is an executive of a large national corporation, and a permanent deacon of the Diocese of Dallas, tells how in his life joy and praise spring from the gift of tears:

Each time I meditate before the crucifix or am deeply in an attitude of mental prayer, a phenomenal experience takes place. My whole being seems to pour out in a flood of tears. I feel the momentary purification of myself, as if the tears were washing away every impurity of my being. For a few moments I feel the inpouring of the Spirit or shall I say the possession of my total being by the

211

Holy Spirit. The immediate reaction is to cry out in joy, the exuberance to praise God at the top of my voice.

The joy of tears comes when I am in prayerful preparation, and yet not expecting it. In my meditation, when I place myself in one of the many gospel scenes and witness the events happening in the life of Christ, I cry out: "Oh, how can this be, have I been one of the causes for the non-acceptance of our Savior in so many lives? Am I worthy to have Jesus as my Master?"

The remorse turns me to sorrow and to beg for forgiveness. The flood of tears takes place again, and it is like being lifted from myself; and to be able to say to my God, "I am yours, accept me as I am, and thank you O Lord for washing me with 'your' tears."

"My eyes flow without ceasing, without respite, until the Lord looks down from heaven and sees" (Lam.3:49-50).

CHAPTER TWENTY-SIX

Praising with Uplifted Arms

In charismatic prayer communities, loud acclamations of the Lord are usually accompanied by uplifted arms, outstretched to welcome the Lord. The psalms have many references to this way of praying. "I will lift up my hands and call on your name" (Ps.63:4). "Lift up your hands to the holy place, and bless the Lord!" (Ps.134:2). One of the more common Hebrew words for praise, *yadah*, "to proclaim, to testify, to worship with extended hands," derives from a root meaning "to use the hand."

Charismatics raise their arms in praise, however, not because they have read that biblical people prayed in that way, but because they are spontaneously impelled from within to do so. Praise of this kind is experienced in a variety of ways and has a wealth of various meanings, as will be evident from the witnesses we shall present.

One young religious woman described it in this way in a letter:

At our Friday evening prayer meeting, we all broke

213

out into spontaneous applause, cheering the risen Lord. We experienced his presence so powerfully! Then at Sunday Mass again I wanted so much to raise my hands to the Lord, but that would be "out of place" in our religious community. Maybe someday we will have communities who are really free to trust one another and pray spontaneously together.

This letter expresses the most common reason for outstretched arms: spontaneous acclamation of the Lord and joyous welcome of his presence.

Those who get up enough courage to let themselves go and raise their arms in prayer find that it brings them a remarkable freedom from the self-consciousness and inhibitions which are always an obstacle to prayer. The act of humility involved in publicly making a fool of oneself of raising the arms in prayer wins this grace of freedom from self-consciousness. The same young woman writes in her letter:

I have been feeling more and more deeply the presence of the Holy Spirit and the freedom to pray without fear or self-consciousness, the freedom to be absolutely at home in praying out loud with others: no fears, no consciousness of self only the total undivided attention to and acclamation of the Lord, without worrying about what others are thinking.

Others have discovered that when they forget themselves and lift up their arms to the Lord, they experience a new freedom from their worries and burdens. "When we lift our arms in praise," they say, "the Lord lifts our burdens from us." "Blessed day by day be the Lord, who bears our burdens" (Ps.68:20n). Praising God in times of trouble by expressing complete trust in him enables us to bear our burdens with love and joy, without being weighed down with anxiety "Do not be grieved, for the joy of the Lord is your strength" (Neh. 8:10).

Uplifted arms signify not only the surrender of our worries to the Lord, they express the yielding of our very self to him in loving and joyous surrender. The young woman already quoted wrote another letter a few months later which manifests a great deepening of her experience of the Lord's presence as she lifts her arms to him. She who had been welcoming him with outstretched arms was now drawn to himself by his outstretched arms:

> *For the first time in my life I stretched out my arms to embrace Jesus on the cross, and he drew me to himself. And it seemed that suffering the cross is not really suffering, but union consummated. The only suffering is to be separated from him, and every other suffering is only intimate union with him. I found myself for the first time begging our Lord to let me share fully in his cross, to let me love it. And then it was as if he said to me, "I want everything. You are mine!"*

Thus, outstretched arms should express a total Yes to the Lord, a wholehearted Amen to his call.

When the joy of acclaim and welcome to the Lord subsides, and the vocal praise quiets into silent adoration, the outstretched arms of welcome are lowered, and are now held in the *deisis* posture of the Russian ikons: the arms are stretched out only from the elbows, which remain at one's side, as when one is receiving an infant into his arms. In this position, the arms express receptivity and adoration, the adoration which is expectant openness to whatever the Lord wills to give, but especially the gift of deeply interior prayer. The same young woman wrote in her first letter: "Interior contemplative prayer flows from spoken praise. Often I just want to be silent the rest of the meeting."

Another woman's testimony tells of a variety of blessings which came to her when she began to praise God aloud with uplifted arms. She is a married woman, the mother of several children, a college graduate and a teacher, and for many years she taught Sunday school in a Baptist church. One day she phoned me and ask if she could come to speak with me, to tell me what praise of God had done in her life. Here is her witness, as well as I could take it down as she spoke:

When I first came to the charismatic prayer meetings and heard everyone praising God loudly with uplifted hands, I was still in the prison of my self-consciousness. I had always "contained" God in my thought processes. I had my ideas about him, but I had never had any existential experience of the Lord's presence. I had sung hymns, but my praise of God was only verbal, and my God was limited to the words. Even when I began to praise God aloud and to lift my hands to him at the prayer meetings, I was still hampered by my self-consciousness, worrying about whether I was praising loudly enough or raising my hands high enough.

But a new freedom came to me as I began to obey the Lord; for I now knew that I must praise loudly and raise my hands in obedience to him. He was calling me to it. This involved a great self-humiliation, but in humbling myself I was at last freed from self-consciousness, and came to the practice of the presence of God. I was released from the hell of self-consciousness to the consciousness of God. I received not just a release of the ability to praise, but also the emergence from my self-consciousness, and I felt young for the first time in my life.

All the newness of God poured into the old dead shell which was me. All my life I had been an old woman, even in my early childhood. Now, for the first time in my life, at the age of fifty, I was a child at last! I felt like taking a tambourine and singing and dancing!

From earliest childhood I had always been filled with fear and anxiety. When I did have a conversion to the Lord at about the age of sixteen, and avidly began to study the Scriptures, I soon found myself imprisoned in systematization. I was forever reasoning, memorizing, categorizing. I built up my structured knowledge about God, and thus hampered my ability to know God. And I became self-righteous, condemning everyone whose religion did not correspond to the religious concepts which I had built up for myself. I thought I was serving the Lord, teaching my theology to others. But I was on the outside, standing outside the Lord and outside those whom I wanted to lead to him. But now that I am free of my prison of self-consciousness, I find that I

*am becoming a "sacrament" of God. I find that he
is living in me, his life is entering into me, and he is
present in me, working in me to draw others to
himself. He is filling me with himself and with a
marvelous love of others as my brothers and sisters
in the Lord.*

*For in praising God I was opened at last to his
love and life. Formerly I was unable to accept
God's love, and was forever blaming myself for
being as I was. But praising him with uplifted arms
I have an experience of timelessness. The Lord
moved through the room where I was.*

*Praising him and raising my hands to him is
abandoning myself to him. In praising God, at last I
can trust me to God!*

In the evening of the day on which I wrote this
chapter, I went to our prayer meeting. In one of the
prophecies, the Lord said, "When I hung on the cross,
my arms were outstretched in continuing praise of my
Father." The Lord's perfect praise was his loving obedience, even unto death. He did not lower his arms, but
willingly allowed them to be nailed to the cross, and he
kept them there till the end.

St. Augustine has a little commentary on the words of
the psalm, "In your name I will lift up my hands"
(Ps.62:4) He writes:

> Raise your hands in prayer. Our Lord raised his
> hands for us on the cross, and they were stretched
> out for us. If on the cross he stretched out his
> hands, it is so that our hands will stretch out in
> doing good works, for his cross has gained us his

mercy. He has raised his hands and offered his very person for us to God in sacrifice, a sacrifice by which all our sins have been wiped out. (On Ps.62, n.14)

Raising the hands in prayer is an offering of self to God. It is a yielding of self to the crucified Lord in his service. As he showed mercy to us, we offer ourselves in mercy to others. By our uplifted arms, we express our great Amen to his call. We reach out our arms to embrace our crucified Lord, and to receive his embrace.

CHAPTER TWENTY-SEVEN

Praise: Weapon in the Spiritual Combat

In reading the testimonies of my friends concerning praise, I noticed a theme emerging: praise is a weapon in the spiritual battle. Most of my friends who praise God without restraint experience this praise as complete surrender to the Lord, as a breaking down of the walls of self-consciousness and of resistance to God, and as a complete acceptance of him as Lord of their lives.

Sometimes this is a conversion from very sinful lives; at other times it is a turning from indifference and lethargy to ardent love and zeal in God's service; sometimes it is a breakthrough from a dark tunnel of seeking and groping into the light and joy of God. It is different for each one, for each human person is unique.

The Lord wins the initial victory in the spiritual combat when we surrender our lives to him in a total commitment. But at that moment, the warfare has really only begun. The surrender to the Lord's love and presence which takes place in praise needs to be repeated again and again in our lives, for Christian living is a continuing combat. Sometimes it is a struggle in which we again resist the Lord; sometimes it is a war against temptation; sometimes a battle in which we carry on the Lord's own warfare in winning others for himself. And therefore praise as a weapon in the personal spiritual combat has been experienced by my friends in a variety of ways.

Weapon Against Difficulties in Prayer

One man, a top executive in a Texas energy corporation, tells of his experience of praise as a joyous surrender to the Lord, who thus had a first victory in this man's spiritual struggle with him:

> When I first came to a charismatic prayer meeting I was, like most conservatively educated Catholics, "turned off" by the praising that I saw and heard. But since my wife and I were truly searching for something to cure the problems in our life, we were willing to try anything. We raised our hands in praise to the Lord during our second prayer meeting, and found in the songs the ability to really give ourselves to the Lord. Through song and the raising of our hands, we found true release and abandon of our hearts to the Lord. I remember that for the first time I truly felt that I was surrendering myself to worship. I realized that the word "worship" had taken on real meaning; before that, it had just been a word.

The man went on to describe in detail the wonderful ease and joy he found in praising the Lord in the days and months that followed. But then came the periods of spiritual dryness when prayer again became a struggle:

Sometimes I have neglected my personal prayer life. And sometimes either through my own fault, or through the Lord's design for my life, I find it difficult to find him in prayer and touch the hem of his robe. However, if I can bring myself, through the grace of his Spirit, to praise him and sing his glory through a conscious act of will, he will bring himself to me and touch my heart. Praise Jesus for his love!

He also found relief from deep discouragement by praising God:

Once when I was in Saudi Arabia on business, I felt very depressed by the difficulty of our negotiations there, the silence of the hotel I was staying at, and the oppressiveness of the city I was in, where every man's mind and heart seemed totally opposed to Jesus Christ and to those who profess him as Lord. I got on my knees and began praying quietly to the Lord in "private prayer," but was soon led to pray in tongues in the Spirit. Soon I raised my arms and started singing in tongues, and then switched to singing some of our prayer meeting songs. I stood up and praised the Lord in a loud voice, rejoicing in the name of "Jesus" uttered aloud in that place. Praise and worship of the Lord and the joy of his Holy Spirit filled my heart and being, and within the space of a few minutes my depression was replaced by that exultant joy. This joy increased to higher and higher levels for about an hour and a half. Praise God! I have never been so upborne.

The name "Jesus" brought great joy to this Texan in the land of the Moslems.

Weapon Against Discouragement

One evening at our prayer meeting, a young man, newlywed, stood up to tell about a beautiful blessing he had received in praising God. He had been driving along the highway, feeling profoundly depressed because of the frightening world situation and because of his worry about his and his wife's future. Then he began to repeat the name *Jesus* over and over. Soon he was praying and singing in tongues. Thus he was opened to receive the Lord's joy, which filled his heart.

This man and his wife, along with another newlywed couple, taught our community to sing the song, "The Joy of the Lord is My Strength" (cf.,Neh.8:10). I always associate that song with them, and am grateful that the Lord is giving our young people "a future full of hope" (Jer.29:11n).

Praise as a struggle is the special characteristic of the lamentation psalms, as we have seen. In these psalms, the praying person struggles against discouragement and despair, he struggles to trust in God. By praising the Lord, his trust grows, and peace and joy fill his heart. Thus the Scriptures prescribe praise of God for every difficult situation, the praise which increases trust, the trust which itself is praise.

223

Weapon Against Temptation

One of the leaders of our community, a business man who has experienced the struggle to carry on business in a Christian way, says, "When I am tempted to return to the ways of my old life, I find freedom from temptation when I begin to praise God. Sometimes, however, the temptation is so attractive that I do not find it easy to praise. Yet through perseverance in praise I win the victory."

Weapon Against Self-Pity

One of our young men who still seems to be struggling with the frustrations and resentments acquired during a difficult childhood, is gradually overcoming them in a continuing spiritual struggle. He wrote this:

> *Often when I am feeling depressed, guilty, sorry for myself, or bearing some resentment towards another person, I begin to praise the Lord in a wholehearted way, and those feelings leave me. I praise the Lord for teaching me of his great love, and how I can experience it through praise. The ability to praise him frees my spirit so that I can listen to Jesus' gentle voice speaking in my heart. It breaks down the walls that I build up around me, so that the Lord can come in, just as in the battle of Jericho the people began to shout their praise of Yahweh, and the walls fell down.*
>
> *The more I praise the Lord with complete*

abandonment, the faster those walls fall down. When I praise him aloud, not caring how much of a fool I make of myself, I can feel a release in my spirit and I can rise to be with Jesus, my love.

Praise in Darkness: "Jesus!"

The name of Jesus, we have seen, brought great joy to the Texas oil man in the land of the Moslems. Here is another witness to the power of that name in winning the spiritual combat. It is from a woman who had often experienced exultant joy in praising the Lord in the days when she first learned the power of praise. But now she tells of a more recent experience of a different kind of praise, praise in the midst of severe trials. This time her praise was a painful struggle out of darkness into joy:

> *Due to a severe financial pressure, I was experiencing heavy, difficult oppression. It was the most severe depression I have ever experienced in my entire life. It was so heavy that literally I could not pray. It was black. I found myself prostrate on the floor desiring God's consolation because of my soul's misery. I did not feel God's presence and knew that all I could say was the name of Jesus. It was the only means of relief and I could barely manage one word—Jesus, Jesus, Jesus. The Jesus prayer was not a real prayer—more automatic sighing for relief from dark depression.*
>
> *For some time I lay on the floor sighing "Jesus." It continued, became louder, began to penetrate my consciousness. I felt the black turn to gray, the*

225

Jesus prayer turning to praying in the Spirit and praising God. And I sensed that I was lying not on the floor but rather on the breast of my Father. I experienced for the first time a love for God the Father not in the abstract as a concept, but I was lying against the real breast of a person—my Father. He was physically close. He loved me personally. I sensed his comfort, his love, his concern.

It was as if God my Father was physically rocking, stroking, patting me as I had been as a child. It was a physical as well as a spiritual presence. It was as if he let me know inside, "I am your Daddy, I know, I understand, I love, I make a difference." I continued to praise God as a child would sob on her daddy's chest. It was a purging and catharsis, a filling not with a solution, but rather a filling of the presence of my Daddy God who overshadowed the problem. It no longer mattered that I receive a solution! I just never wanted to be removed from the physical presence of the sweetness of my Daddy God.

For the first time in my life I experienced the love and the personal, physical presence of God the Father.

I knew that something deep inside was changed in such a way that I was healed, made whole. I really can't explain in human words what happened exactly, but after the experience of praising God I received his comfort and consolation in such a way that for the first time I loved God the Father and my earthly father with a God-given love, and this love and presence continues to live within me.

226

A Nun's Witness

A cloistered nun also has given witness concerning the praise which is sheer faith, the faith which continues to seek even when there are no signs of God's presence. Speaking from long experience in contemplative prayer, she wrote, "To praise him in pure faith is a reality." She is referring to the spiritual dryness in which praise does not bubble forth spontaneously and freely. Yet, continuing attention to the Lord in pure faith is true praise, for to be faithful in seeking him when he is difficult to find is certainly to appreciate him greatly. There is also a genuine form of praise which calmly, deliberately, sincerely praises God in pure faith without any exuberance of feeling. The profound depth of such faith could make this praise far more valuable than the enthusiastic bubbling praise of a beginner, whose faith has not yet deepened in the test of time and trials.

This nun speaks also of "praise" versus "love." She did not really mean that there is opposition between praise and love. She was speaking of a silent praise which is pure love, without any other expression except itself. Instead of reacting with expressions of praise when she experiences the love and beauty and goodness of God in a contemplative way, she reacts purely with love. The love itself is praise enough.

Touching God in Faith

The spiritual combat often takes the form of a battle through to God in the darkness of faith. The following words have been very helpful to one of my friends who has lived faithfully with the Lord, even though she has been granted few of those signs of his love and presence which make so many of her friends exuberant in praise.

We burst into joyous praise of God whenever he grants us a favor: a healing or a vision, a manifestation of his closeness or an experience of consolation in his presence, a prophetic word of love addressed to our praying community or a touch of his presence in our inner being. But our deeper, underlying, ever-enduring motive for praise is his ever-enduring, ever-present, ever-active steadfast love and faithfulness, whether we are having an experience of this love or not. We know in faith that it is there, even when we do not feel it or see striking signs of it.

It is this ever present and saving God whom we reach and touch in faith. We touch God himself in faith, we reach him directly. We touch him in faith even without the mediation of the various signs of his presence. Particular favors, such as this vision or that physical healing, this experience of his closeness or that consolation in prayer, should not be dwelt upon as though they were the whole Christian reality. They should rather be accepted gratefully, when God sees fit to give them, as signs of the deeper reality, namely, the steadfast, faithful presence of God with us. "Unless you see signs and wonders, you will not believe," complained Jesus (John 4:48). People tend to stop at the signs and miss the deeper reality to which they point: God himself present in our midst giving life and salvation.

Even in the dryness and darkness of faith we are united directly to this God, when we seek him perseveringly in steadfast trust. When we are given no words, no visions, no physical healings, no taste of his sweetness and favor, we are nonetheless united directly to him in ordinary faith, hope and love, and complete trust in his ordinary providence. The reality is infinitely greater than the sign. When the sign is withheld by the Lord, we accept and expect the greater reality just the same. For example, when no miracle of physical healing is granted when we ask for it, in faith we nonetheless receive the Lord himself, and deeper divine life in him.

There are Christians who never receive visions or words from the Lord, yet who are more intimately united with him in faith and love than are some other people who do receive these words and visions and healings. "Without having seen him you love him; though you do not now see him you believe in him and rejoice with unutterable and exalted joy" (1 Pet.1:8).

The deeper, ever-abiding motive for Christian joy and praise is God's steadfast presence with us in the person of the risen Lord Jesus. This presence is summed up in the meaning of the name Jesus: "Yahweh is our ever-present, ever-acting salvation."

CHAPTER TWENTY-EIGHT

Praise as a Weapon against Satan

By his nature, Satan is a liar and a blasphemer. His lying insinuations against God are a blasphemous insult to God's glory. The beast in the Book of Revelations is a front for Satan, and he is described as having a blasphemous mouth. "The beast was given a mouth for uttering proud boasts and blasphemies.... It began to hurl blasphemies against God, reviling him and the members of his heavenly household as well" (Rev.13:5n).

The beast symbolizes the powers of evil incarnate in those human power structures which are in opposition to God and which usurp God's prerogatives. "On its horns were ten diadems and on its heads blasphemous names" (Rev.13:1n).

Indeed, Satan and the two beasts are a caricature of the Holy Trinity. The first beast imitated the risen Lord (Rev.13:3). The second beast, by the wonders he works, mimics the Holy Spirit who works miracles in the Church to encourage faith in Christ (Rev.13:13-14). Just as the Son of God had become incarnate in human nature and in the members of his body, the Church, and in this body exercises the power of the Holy Spirit, so Satan's evil power is incarnate in those human political, economic and social structures which are not according to God. By this power the beast arouses amazement in the hearts of men, which leads to worship of the beast. The second beast is the lying propaganda system of the evil power structure, and wins a religious cult for the beast. For the evil power structure is feared and worshipped as though it were a god: "Who is like the beast, and who can fight against it?" (Rev.13:4).

The whole history of mankind is the story of Satan's struggle against God, a struggle which is incarnate in the struggles of men to build and maintain their selfish power structures. The beast is reincarnated in one evil power system after another. This is symbolized by the fact that the beast combines in himself the features of the various beasts which symbolized the successive empires which fought against God and his people in the Book of Daniel. He has the nimbleness of a leopard, the strength of a bear and the great mouth of a lion (compare Rev.13:1-2 with Daniel 7:3-8). He is the inhuman form of degenerate political power.

Men are always being deceived into making the beast their god: "Who is like the beast, and who can fight against it?" They are easily enslaved by fear of the beast, fear of the death and other evils he can inflict upon them in his marvelous power, fear that he will deprive them of thé things they need and desire (Rev.13:15-17).

Who is Like God?

The acclaim given the beast and the subservient fear of

231

his power—"Who is like the beast, and who can fight against it?"—is a perversion of the loving and joyful worship of the true God expressed in the psalms. The worship of Yahweh in the Old Testament is characterized by joyous confidence and loving praise of his magnificent, astounding power, for in steadfast love and faithfulness to his promises he uses that power to save his people and bring them home to his presence:

> *Who is like to you* among the gods, O Lord? Who is like to you, magnificent in holiness? O terrible in renown, worker of wonders. . . . In your mercy you led the people you redeemed; in your strength you guided them to your holy dwelling (Exod.15: 11-13n).

The worship of the beast, on the contrary, is a joyless fear, a despairing, hopeless capitulation to him: *"Who is like the beast, and who can fight against it?"*

But worship of the true God brings joy and salvation: "But I will rejoice in the Lord, I will be joyful because of his salvation. All my being shall say, 'O Lord, *who is like you*, the rescuer of the afflicted man from those too strong for him?' " (Ps.35:9-10n).

He defends and rescues the poor and the oppressed: *"Who is like the Lord our God*, who is enthroned on high?. . . He raises up the lowly from the dust; from the dungheap he lifts up the poor" (Ps.113:5-7n). He is forever faithful to his promises, and uses his wonderful power in fulfilling them: "O Lord, God of hosts, *who is like you?* Mighty are you, O Lord, and your faithfulness surrounds you" (Ps.89:9n).

The beast, on the contrary, by his awesome power and

wonders, inspires a worship which is essentially an enslaving fear, bringing man into bondage to Satan. The Son of God came to free us from this fear. "Jesus likewise had a full share in our flesh and blood, that by his death he might rob the devil, the prince of death, of his power, and free those who through fear of death had been slaves their whole life long" (Heb.2:14-15n).

Sincere praise of God, "O Lord, who is like you?" (Ps.35:10n), destroys the blasphemous worship of the beast, "who is like the beast?" The Book of Revelation is like one great liturgy of praise of God and of the Lamb, nullifying the worship of the beast. The victory songs to the Lamb and to Him who sits on the throne counteract the fear of the beast and of death. "The Lamb standing as if slain" (Rev.5:6) is victorious over death, and death is not defeat for those who suffer and die in witness to him:

> Worthy is the Lamb that was slain to receive power and riches, wisdom and strength, honor and glory and praise.... To the One seated on the throne, and to the Lamb, be praise and honor, glory and might, forever and ever! ... Now have salvation and power come, the reign of our God and the authority of his Anointed One. For the accuser of our brothers is cast out, who night and day accused them before our God. They defeated him by the blood of the Lamb and by the word of their testimony; love for life did not deter them from death" (Rev.5:12-13; 12:10-11n).

"The accuser of our brothers" tries to stir up fear and self-condemnation in the hearts of men, for discouragement over our failings is one of Satan's best weapons against us. But discouragement and despair are counteracted by praise of the Lamb and by accepting forgiveness and reconciliation in his blood.

The very name of Michael, the angel who defeats the dragon and casts him from heaven, is a symbol of praise, the weapon by which the powers of evil are conquered. Michael means "Who is like God?" and directly counteracts the blasphemous claims of Satan and the beast, "Who is like the beast?" Praise is the battleground on which Satan is defeated. The whole person of Michael cries out, "Who is like God," for Michael is totally submissive to God in humble obedience and service. Every true follower of Christ is a Michael, for his whole person and way of life bears witness to the Lord and glorifies him as God.

Honoring Satan

We have noted how we all tend to blame everyone but ourselves for our sins and miseries. Adam blamed Eve and Eve blamed Satan. The tendency to blame Satan for everything is dangerous, for it can be a way of honoring Satan by attributing to him powers which the Lord has taken away from him. It is a paying of homage to a power which Christ has broken, a power which enslaves only those who remain in their sins. Blaming the devil for everything is giving honor where honor is not due. Blaming Satan can be a way of failing to admit our own guilt in a matter. It can be an abdication of our personal responsibility for our sins, which could be overcome by the Lord's redeeming power.

We should not honor Satan by "witnessing" unduly to his all-pervading influence. Satan is best defeated by despising him and witnessing rather to the power of Christ which has conquered him. I honor Christ and his power by choosing Christ and implementing that choice in my whole life by living in his power and Spirit. I honor Jesus as Lord, and thus ignore Satan and render him powerless, by accepting Jesus as Lord of my life. I do this by fulfilling my personal responsibilities according to his will and becoming what he calls me to be. I praise the Lord and glorify him by walking in the ways he has prepared for me. I do this, of course, by his power and Spirit.

To exaggerate unduly the power and influence of Satan is to blaspheme the Lord by implying that he is not really Lord, since his power is so diluted by Satan's power. To see Satan at work everywhere and in everything is to honor the beast: "Who is like the beast, and who can resist him?"

Attributing every little failure in our life to Satan is to shirk our own responsibility for many of these failings. To exaggerate Satan's influence is like saying that the Lord is powerless to help his people. Satan loves to stir up doubts about the Lord's power and willingness to help us. He insinuates that the Lord is not concerned about us: "Where is your God?" (Ps.42:3). To doubt the Lord's power or willingness to help is to doubt that he is Lord.

We are God's children, not frightened slaves of Satan and the beast. "For you did not receive the spirit of slavery to fall back into fear, but you have received the spirit of sonship" (Rom.8:15). As God's children, we accept responsibility for our lives, taking full blame for our own sinfulness, confessing our sins and by the grace of Christ changing our ways. Even if Satan does work in our lives by tempting us, he has a victory only when we shirk our responsibility to let Jesus be our Lord by walking in his ways. If we say Yes to the Lord by living in him, we have no need to honor Satan by fearing him.

CHAPTER TWENTY-NINE

Incipient Mysticism

In the early days of the Catholic charismatic renewal, someone said about the charismatics: "These people are looking for instant mysticism. They expect God to do everything in their lives in a miraculous way. They expect God to give them the fullness of holiness on a silver platter. They know nothing about the spiritual combat, the long struggle to the heights of holiness."

In my experience, however, seasoned charismatics are very aware indeed of the spiritual combat, because they are so deeply involved in it on so many different levels. But they do have a most effective weapon for the combat: an unshakeable, expectant hope. They expect the Lord to do marvels in their lives, and they express this expectation in joyous praise of the risen Lord. And he does do wonderful things in their lives. But not without their cooperation, as they carry on the struggle for holiness.

A friend has recently described the charismatic renewal not as instant mysticism, but as *incipient mysticism*. In other words, there are many elements of authentic mysticism manifest in the renewal, though for the most part this mysticism is still in its beginnings. But because of the sincerity and simplicity of their surrender of themselves to the Lord in expectant trust, the charismatics are indeed remarkably open to the working of the Holy Spirit. Therefore it is to be expected that he will ripen many of the mystical fruits in them. "By their fruits you shall know them." I have seen much of this fruit already appearing.

The way the charismatics surrender themselves to the Lord in enthusiastic praise is often criticized as being too emotional, and therefore as anything but mystical. Those who make this objection, however, have the notion that true mysticism requires complete death to the human and the emotional. They consider, moreover, that the loud praising of the charismatics is as primitive as David's ecstatic dancing before the ark of the covenant, or as primitive as the *teruwah*, the battle cry in the presence of the ark.

However, at a typical charismatic prayer meeting, with its loud joyful praising, its uplifted arms, and its occasional dancing in the Spirit, there are certainly elements of authentic mysticism, even though some of these manifestations may indeed seem primitive. But by their fruits you shall know them. The fruits of conversion and holiness that are so manifest in the lives of so many of these people are the undeniable proof that God is with them and has made himself known to them. At times, the whole praying community is intensely aware of the presence of God, and God is truly manifesting himself in their midst.

In the midst of the enthusiastic acclamation of the Lord's presence, a certain percentage of the people may indeed be experiencing that presence in a very primitive way, and their shouts of joy may be on the same level as the Israelite war cry. Some may indeed be very inexperienced beginners in the spiritual warfare. But the Lord *has* touched them, and his touch is an invitation to go on to the very peaks of the spiritual life. Their incipient mysticism is frequently deeply authentic.

In the same enthusiastic group, others may well be experiencing the divine presence in a more profound way, in graces of deep recollection or in gifts of infused contemplation. I know of a sizeable number of cases in which this is so.

And there are many other levels of experience of God in between the "primitives" and the more advanced contemplatives. The ways of the Holy Spirit are diverse, and he leads his people in a multitude of authentic ways.

The incipient mysticism touches not only purified souls who, through long continuing personal discipline, are well disposed for deeper graces of prayer. It touches sinners also. Their resultant conversion is the fruit of a touch of the Holy Spirit, and any such touch belongs in the realm of mystical grace.

Any authentic touch of God's Spirit given in the midst of enthusiastic praise is an invitation to conversion. But some who have received the touch do not respond to the invitation; or if they do, they sometimes fall away again. But the fact that some do not change their ways after they have joined in praise does not necessarily prove that they had no experience at all of the Lord's presence. It may mean that they did not accept the invitation contained in the touch of his grace.

There is a type of person who continues to attend prayer meetings, and enthusiastically cries out in words to the Lord, but whose praise is not fully sincere. He

239

may indeed have received an initial touch of the Lord, but has not followed it up by deeply changing his ways. He continues his hymn singing as a kind of pseudo-religion, a religiosity that camouflages his moral disorders from himself. Because he sings hymns, his conscience is soothed. He may even become quite fanatical in promoting religion, but his fanaticism is only a mask for his disorderly life.

For everyone who receives it, the grace of praise is an invitation to continuing conversion. The initial response to the Lord must be completed in full conversion. But conversion is an on-going process, as the old self is gradually put to death and the new self comes alive ever more fully in the risen Lord. The sign of the authenticity of the mystical touch in the lives of charismatics is not perfection already at its consummation, but genuine striving towards that perfection.

Therefore in evaluating something like the charismatic renewal, we should take into consideration the positive good fruits already in evidence, and not simply the failings and weaknesses of people who are still "a pilgrim people" on the way. Authentic mystical graces are in evidence in a group which also has the weaknesses which are so common in all the people of God.

Because these weaknesses are still there, the Lord repeatedly invites the people to a continuing and deeper conversion, and growth in ever wider areas of Christian living and apostolate and social action. God is praised by righteousness of life. "Praise" and "the right way" are presented as synonyms in parallel lines in a psalm: "He that offers *praise* as a sacrifice glorifies me, and to him that goes *the right way* I will show the salvation of God" (Ps.50:23n). Living in the right way is thus the sacrifice of praise which glorifies the Lord, and opens his people to receive "the glory" which is his saving presence.

Thus, the test of our sincerity in praising God is our sincerity in striving for an ever more complete change of our ways from sinfulness to holiness. "Praise is unseemly in a sinner's mouth, since it has not been put there by the Lord. For true praise is expressed in wisdom, and it is the Lord who guides it" (Sir.15:9-10*b*). Wisdom is not simply concepts in the mind, it is right living in practice.

A Well-Tuned Life

The gift of praise given by the Lord is always an invitation to an ever more complete conversion to him, lest there be discord in the music played by the Holy Spirit in our lives. A disorderly life is out of tune. It is in disharmony with our words of praise, and merits the Lord's condemnation, "This people honors me with their lips, but their heart is far from me" (Matt.15:8).

Sister Elizabeth of the Trinity, who called herself "Praise of His Glory" (Eph.1:14) to express her vocation to *be* the praise of God in the totality of her life, speaks of the Christian's life as a lyre played by God to bring forth divine music for his glory:

But the lyre is not in tune, and the Master cannot draw forth divine harmonies from it, unless a person's whole being is kept in unity by interior silence, seeking but the one thing necessary: the Lord himself (Luke 10:42). All one's powers must be collected into unity by being occupied in the one work of love, having the 'single eye' (Luke 11:34) which allows God's light to enlighten us. If one's powers are scattered in self-seeking, then one cannot be a perfect "Praise of Glory," one is unfit to sing the great song of which St. Paul speaks (Eph.1:14) because he is not in unity and order. When a person's life is not unified by seeking the Lord alone, instead of persevering in praise in simplicity whatever may happen, that person must be continually tuning the strings of his instrument, which are all a little off key.[49]

His life is not collected into perfect unity by love. By praising the Lord in every situation, in acceptance of his loving purposes, one's life is brought into ever more perfect tune with the Holy Spirit, and he makes that life a beautiful melody in praise of God, for the encouragement and edification of all who see it.

Dancing With God

One day Jesus complained about people's unresponsiveness to his word by telling a homely little parable about children who always want to play some other game than the one suggested by their companions: "What comparison can I use to describe this breed? They are like children squatting in the town squares, calling to their playmates: 'We piped you a tune but you did not dance! We sang you a dirge but you did not wail!' " (Matt.11:16-17n).

Elizabeth of the Trinity spoke of the life of praise in terms of a well-tuned lyre perfectly responsive to the Holy Spirit. Madeleine Delbrel has expressed it magnificently in terms of dancing with God in perfect responsiveness to his leading:

If there are many good people who do not like to dance, there are many saints who felt it necessary to dance because they enjoyed life so very much. There was Theresa with her castanets, St. John of the Cross with a statue of the Infant Jesus in his arms, and St. Francis before the pope. If we were pleased with you, Lord, we would not be able to resist this urge to dance which is world-wide. And we would come to know which dance you want us to engage in by following the lead of your Providence.

I think that you are perhaps rather tired of people who want to serve you always with the manners of captains, to know you after the manner of professors, to reach you with rules of sport, to love you as an aged couple love each other.

One day when you desired something different, you devised St. Francis, and made him a jongleur. We should let ourselves be devised so as to be joyful people who dance their life with you.

To be a good dancer, with you or with others, it is not necessary to know where the dance leads. It is necessary to follow, to be gay, to be light, and most of all not to be stiff. We should not ask you to explain what steps you are pleased to take. We must be like a prolongation, agile and living with you, and through you we must receive the transmission of the rhythm of the orchestra. We must not wish at any cost to go forward, but accept to turn, to go sideways. We must know how to stop and slide instead of walking. And these would be only foolish steps, if they were not to be in harmony with the music.

But we forget the music of your Spirit, and we

243

make our life an exercise of gymnastics. We forget that in your arms, life is danced, and that your holy will is an inconceivable fantasia, and that there is no monotony and boredom except for those oldsters who choose to be wallflowers at the joyful ball of your love.

Lord, come and invite us. We are ready to dance for you that errand we have to make, those accounts, the dinner we must prepare, that watch we have to keep when we feel sleepy. We are prepared to dance the dance of labor for you, the dance of heat, and later that of cold. If certain tunes are in minor we shall not tell you they are sad. If others make us breathe hard, we shall not say they make us breathless. And if some persons barge into us we shall take it laughingly, knowing well that this always happens in a dance.

Lord, teach us what place is taken by the singular ball of our obedience in that eternal romance begun between you and us.[50]

A life which is danced in such perfect unison with the Lord occasionally breaks forth into literal dancing for joy. Marie of the Incarnation, the holy Canadian Ursuline nun (died 1672), tells us that "in an inexpressible exuberance, she experienced powerful movements of leaping and clapping her hands, and calling upon the whole world to sing the praises of a God so great" (DS 8:1477).

This is jubilation of the kind described by St. Augustine. It is an expression of profound mystical grace, not a mere primitive emotional enthusiasm. Authentic mysticism has its overflow into all the powers of body and spirit.

PART FIVE

A Song
for the Lord Alone

CHAPTER THIRTY

Adoration is Praise

"My way of praising God is contemplation." A cloistered Dominican nun spoke these words to me when I asked her what praise means in her life. Her few additional words can be summed up in this way: "Of all the forms which praise takes in my life, contemplation is the richest and fullest."

Most people tend to think of praise only in terms of heartfelt song and expressive poetic words, but associate contemplation with silence, solitude, and wordless adoration, How then can silent contemplation be praise? Can praise be expressed by silence?

The etymology of the word "praise" gives a clue for answering these questions.

"Praise" is derived from late Latin *pretiare*, "to prize," which, in turn, derives from *pretium*, "price." To prize something is to value it highly, to appreciate it. The word "appreciate," too, comes from *pretium*.

Appreciation is an essential element of all sincere praise. To praise is to detect a value, to appreciate it, and to express this appreciation. The most common way

247

of expressing loving appreciation is by word or song. We have seen also how praise of God is expressed by the way we live, showing our loving appreciation of him in all of our actions. But silent adoration is also praise, for it is one of the most eloquent ways of expressing appreciation of who and what God is. One cannot truly appreciate God without responding to him in loving adoration.

Adoration is the special honor due to God because of his infinite grandeur and majesty as our Creator, our Lord and Ruler, our fulfillment and happiness. True adoration is a willing submission of self to him. It is a loving appreciation and acceptance of him for what he is: our source and our goal, who is lovingly governing us, leading us to himself as our fulfillment and our joy. Adoration is willingly and lovingly belonging to God, that he might fulfill in us the purposes of his creating and redeeming love.

All of this presupposes that we have some knowledge or experience of God and of his majestic grandeur. This knowledge and experience is offered to everyone: "Ever since the creation of the world his invisible nature, namely, his eternal power and deity, has been clearly perceived in the things that have been made" (Rom.1:20). "He is not far from each one of us, for in him we live and move and have our being" (Acts 17:27-28). "The true light ... enlightens every man" (John 1:9).

All authentic praise, whether expressed in word or in song, in life or in service, presupposes such knowledge or experience of God. Indeed, all true praise of God is an expression of adoration. In its deepest essence, praise *is* adoration, for it recognizes, acknowledges, and welcomes God for what he is—the Lord God, "enthroned on the praises of Israel" (Ps.22:3).

Adoration becomes more perfect in the measure that loving knowledge of God becomes more profound, and in the degree that one's will becomes more steadfast in its loving submission to him, more willing in its readiness to serve him in selfless devotion. The more a person lovingly acquiesces in his total dependence upon God, the more profound his adoration will be. Adoration will become a permanent attitude of his whole person, as it was in Jesus Christ our Lord.

Bossuet describes this attitude of permanent adoration:

> It is a certain reverence for God, a desire for him, submission to him, rest in him, complaisance towards him, secret satisfaction in belonging to him, a deep-rooted disposition to see everything in him, and to relate everything to him, to revere what he is, to esteem whatever he wills, always and in every circumstance, it not with feeling, at least in one'· deepest heart. (DS I:219)

Adoration lovingly acknowledges and accepts not onl· what God is in himself, but what he is for us: why he made us, what he wills to do in us, what he wills to be for us. It is the recognition of God's total rights over our whole being. It is a willingness to belong to him as his own. But we are his own because he has created us in love, he has redeemed us in love, he is sanctifying us in love. We belong to him in love and he possesses us in love so that he might give himself totally to us in love.

As response to God's love, adoration in its deepest essence is love's free gift of self to him, to belong to him in wholehearted submission to his loving purposes. It is loving attention to what he wills to do in us and be for us. He desires and deserves our fullest attention as often and as persistently as we can give it to him. He deserves our adoring attention because he is infinitely adorable in his majesty and glory, he is awe-inspiring and wonderful in his glorious beauty and love. He desires our adoring attention, because his love for us wants to fill us with his own happiness and joy, which he shares with us when we participate in the wonders of his divine life.

Adoration, then, is the recognition of God's legitimate hold upon what is deepest in us: our very self. We are his. We deliver up to him our entire being in adoration to belong to him exclusively, in his presence. Adoration is being lovingly wrapped up in God in forgetfulness of self. It is loss to self in attention to God. It is a sort of death to everything that is not God, in total submission to him who is our all.

The truest thing our praise can say is, "My God and my all!" There is no more eloquent way of saying this than by complete silence of the heart in his presence, in order to be attentive to the light and love and life which he wills to pour into our empty and open hearts. Sheer being with him to be filled with his love and presence is a wonderfully complete way of belonging to him. This is the fullness of adoration. It is letting God pour out his presence into our whole being in the graces of infused contemplation. This requires silence to all else. He created and redeemed us in love to be his own. We are his own so that he might fill us with the joy of his presence, the happiness of possessing him in loving communion.

To accept all of this in silent, loving adoration is a most eloquent form of praise. For it is to appreciate and accept God in his deepest essence: "God is love."

God's love is absolutely gratuitous, it is pure giving. "In this is love, not that we loved God, but that he loved us" (1 John 4:10). In the face of this infinite and totally gratuitous divine love, the only possible response is adoring acceptance of love, in silent simplicity.

For there is nothing we can do to merit this love. It cannot be bought with gold or silver, it cannot be earned by all the human achievements in the world, it cannot be enticed by the bringing of gifts, or by the beauty of liturgical song and dance. Love can only be received as gift. The fullness of God's love can be received fully only in the utter simplicity of complete openness in love, and the gift of self in response. In its most developed form, adoration is the quiet simplicity of loving acceptance of God's love.

This is the contemplative attitude. And this is eloquent praise, for to accept his love is the supreme appreciation of God who is love. To appreciate his love is to say Yes to it, to surrender to it, to be a perfect Amen to it. "She must hold the door of her will open to the Bridegroom that he may enter through the complete and true 'Yes' of love."[51]

The most perfect form of adoration and therefore the most magnificent kind of praise is the silent adoration which is total surrender to his love, letting his love have its way in us, letting his love pour himself out to us in infused contemplation, letting him give us "the voice of the nightingale: the new song of jubilation to God sung with God's own voice given to us."[52]

We see then why my friend could say, "Contemplation is my way of praising God." To this she has been called by God.

CHAPTER THIRTY-ONE

Praise in the Monastery

Cloistered nuns from three monasteries responded to my request for witness concerning praise in their lives. These nuns experience the gift of praise in a variety of ways. Some of the responses emphasize praise as interior contemplation, others focus on the liturgical aspects of praise, some experience praise in a charismatic way, one spoke of expressing praise in various art forms, such as painting and poetry, still others praise God in response to their awareness of him in the quiet of nature, the woods, the lakeside, or the hidden grove at the end of the cloister garden.

Some of the responses went into more detail than we can use in this book, so I have summarized two points which received special emphasis from several of the witnesses:

First, they experienced their sacrificial life in the cloister as a living sacrifice of praise, in union with the Lord's own life of praise. One nun wrote, "My 'gifts of praise' are no longer those which are 'apart' from me, but rather, that which is of me, of Jesus living in me."

Secondly, this life of praise is consciously rooted in

252

the sacred liturgy of the Mass and of the liturgical hours of praise. Another nun wrote:

> *The living sacrifice of praise which is my life is consummated in the Eucharistic liturgy, and in the liturgy of the hours, where we express in word and song what we are living in the totality of our lives. My awareness of the Holy Spirit's action in and through the liturgy plunges me ever deeper into the liturgy, where I feel Christ and his Church praying in me and through me. I experience the reality spoken of so well by Vatican II when it says that the Sacred Liturgy "is truly the voice of the Bride addressing her Bridegroom; it is the prayer which Christ himself, together with his body, addresses to the Father."*

The witness of another nun resembles what several charismatic lay people have told me about their personal morning prayer in the quiet of their homes:

> *I begin by morning prayer time (in my cell) with a few moments of quiet song in tongues—a praise type of song, with heart and hands uplifted to God. When the song dies away, I close my eyes—and a beautiful peace envelops my whole being—and I seem to be taken into the heart of the Trinity in a beautiful prayer of quiet—a deep stillness with all distractions just melted away.*

The rest of this chapter is the eloquent witness of a nun whom I have known well for many years. When I decided to use it, I wrote to her asking under what circumstances she had received this gift of praise. In answer, she quoted from a letter she had written to a friend the same day that she received the gift:

> *Yesterday, some charismatic people witnessed to our community. They prayed with us and for us that we too, already living in the Spirit, would receive his fullest outpouring. This morning I was outside before Mass, praying as usual in a secluded spot, praying in whispers and in silence, intent on nothing but God and lifting my hands to him, when his Presence suddenly invaded me and my words changed to words I did not know, except that they were joy and praise and surrender. This lasted only a few minutes, but there was something so different about it from all the prayer that had gone before, that I have no doubt about its meaning. When I had returned to myself enough to reflect on the event, I sat back and said aloud, 'The Lord has baptized me in his Spirit!'*

She wrote that on June 14, 1970. In June, 1975, she wrote the following for this book.

A Nun's Experience of the Gift of Praise

> *(June 10, 1975)*
> *It was the Lord himself who taught me to praise when he poured the anointing of his Spirit over me five years ago in a moment that seemed to stand outside of time. Before it, I was in a desert land, struggling in prayer, afraid of scrifice, in bondage*

to self, weak in my vocation, helpless to heal my wounds. After it, I was a new creation, and to this day the grace, the strength, the healing, the light, the savor of God's Presence abide and continue to grow.

The Lord accomplished all this by drawing a burst of praise from my heart, the only response a creature can give when it has been empty and suddenly knows itself invaded by God. The gift of tongues came to me then, to give release to an inexpressible expansion of my soul trying to respond to God's mystery. Indeed, in the actual experience I did not ask myself what was happening. being powerless except to surrender.

After it subsided a little and I could reflect on its meaning, there came an absolute certainty (in the sense that I have never been able to doubt it) that his Holy Spirit had taken new possession of me by his own will, and that my old life was changed.

Perhaps the most significant thing the Lord did through this new gift of praise that began to well up within me truly as a spring of water, sometimes flowing, sometimes a clear still pool, was a vision and acceptance of my own nothingness, emptiness, sinfulness, helplessness, in which he was doing this wonder. In me, who least deserved his mercy, he chose to accomplish his mercy, so that all who saw it would know that it was his power alone.

When God gave me this gift of praise, I had already been a religious for ten years, and in all that time had seemingly never learned just to give him glory as a form of prayer. What a good teacher the Holy Spirit was! In the weeks and months that followed, my prayer developed into a texture of spoken, whispered, sung, laughing, weeping praise, praise of the body, with uplifted hands, or prostrate, and praise in tongues.

Praise and Contemplation (June 11, 1975)

(June 11, 1975)

More and more I noticed that a prayer period begun in explicit praise would end in silence. Not because there was nothing left to express. Rather, God so often drew so near that praise became an inexpressible possessing of him. I do not know why, when he reveals himself as very, very close, everything within is struck with silence. At least, with me it is so.

It is very clear to me now that this gift of praise was for the sake of a deeper contemplative prayer. Now, the outward expressions of praise when I am alone at prayer are much less, and often not at all. The soul is already in silence. But when it is not still, but distracted, a conscious and from-the-heart expression of praise in whatever form his spirit leads to, has a special power to cleanse and heal my natural weariness, and quickly make a deep prayer spring up.

I do not mean to say that praise now is only a "method to be used." No. Praise is always and only a surrender of my total person to my God. That it also has his divine power within it to gather together the scattered fragments of my human weakness is still another reason to give him glory. Perhaps the reason for this is that praise of my Lord takes all attention away from "self," which is thus left without nourishment and has to die.

Sometimes when God has wanted to take this poor soul as far into himself as it can bear to go, I have seen that praise and prayer seem in me to pass through four levels or periods. First, there is the conscious praise, usually, but not necessarily, expressed. From that flows a silence in which God's presence becomes more and more known. If he chooses to take me so far, the experience will not stop there, but he will embrace me with such strength that I seem to feel my very soul straining to break away from this body so as to be able to receive him fully. Because it is not possible, and because the pain and sweetness together cannot be kept in, the soul and body begin to express it all in sighs, tears, little sounds of pain, burning loving words. I think this would seem a madness if someone should see it. And then God stills it all again and takes my soul one step farther, and for this there is nothing to say because there is no awareness for this little while except that it it held in God.

(June 13, 1975)

There is a praise which cannot be kept in, but it is not a praise of my choosing to utter, it is a response from his own Spirit within my soul when he touches me or draws me or shows me his beauty. How can I say it cannot be kept in, when clearly his Spirit is one of order, and there are times and places, at least in religious life, when one must not be noticed. If he comes in a moment like that,

257

when the glory must remain within, then it will do so, but for a while the awareness and ability to relate to things and persons around can be obscured.

Tomorrow will mark the very day that God poured out his Spirit and taught me to praise, five years ago. In my heart, this grace is as living and new as if it had happened today. For he indwells my heart, and I am sure of it, and he lets me "see" him there, as it were, whenever I turn and look with desire. I know a joy that no one can take away, as he promised. This is the singing in my heart: O my God, you are with me! Once I understood this by faith alone, and that faith is still there. But God has added something more, something wholly gift, a certainty that is a kind of vision. I do not understand how it can be. Only that one day he made me a promise in a special way that he would never hide his face from me. And since that day he has made his home with me. Every day he is new, while every day the same. This is why praise can be endlessly repeated without being wearisome, without ever finishing the story of his goodness. Every other human experience is either completed, or simply left behind by time. This being possessed by God is ever beginning and can never be lost I know I am still free to reject God by sin, serious sin, but that is a freedom I pray I may never use).

It isn't that I do not fail you, O my Lord, I very much know how weak I am, and nothingness. In this poor house of mine you have still desired to dwell and to make it holy. Yes, Jesus, for you my heart must sing.

A Community of Praise

God has drawn me into a community of praise, where we live not only alone for him, but together for him. It would not be enough for one voice, one heart to glorify the Lord. No, all must do it; the fullness of each one's joy must be shared. Sometimes I could be inclined to think that community praise is less perfect or less meaningful for me, because it so seldom leads to the depth-experience that can come so easily when we are alone. How wrong that would be, as if praise were to bring me fulfillment rather than solely to magnify the Lord. And I have come to understand that no one voice could ever, even under the movement of the Holy Spirit, mirror God's greatness even to itself. No, all creation was made to unite in his praise, and his revelation promises that it will be so.

I think it is this way: that my own desire to give my whole being as a sacrifice of praise to God is more kindled in the secret moments that I share with him. And the glory of his power and work in all his people is more radiant when they come together to proclaim that he alone is the God so near his people, the God who is Love.

(June 15,1975)
The Lord has also let me discover that I cannot give voice to my praise, alone, but most especially within the community, unless my heart is upright before him and before them. Praise is a flame of his Spirit, and it must purify my soul or be extin-

259

guished. That is why I had to repent the other evening when God gave me to understand that my openness to the community in love and generosity had lately been far short of what God wanted it to be.

Some may think it strange, but I have seen and known that praise of God, poured out intensely in all the expressions that his people together may give it, reaches a peak at which his presence so takes each heart that they fall silent. And that silence, so full of him, is like a moment of life in the heavenly city.

To me it is not so different, what he works in my soul in solitude, and what he works in my soul in my praying community. In his Word of the Old Testament, the people and the individual always embody each other before him. Under his New Covenant it is the same, more than ever, since now his Spirit truly fills and teaches and exults within all his Body on earth.

Jesus, you are the Lord in whom alone we worship the Father. Be praised then in every heart, perfect your people through your gift of praise until all is ready, and you can present your holy Bride in the Kingdom of your Father. Amen!

Six months later, sister wrote again (December, 1975):

Since I wrote you in June I have been discovering more and more that if praise is, as it were, an open door into prayer, there is something that can lock that door, at least for me. This is self-righteous things that I might be trying to rationalize, like resisting God's will in some circumstances, unforgiveness, interior criticism and/or impatience. I had never seen these things so clearly before as obstacles to the very act of praise. Real sin, repented, is not the problem; but the evil in disguise that I try to justify.

CHAPTER THIRTY-TWO

The Tension between
Vocal Praise and Contemplation

The praise which is contemplation in silent adoration is not the exclusive prerogative of cloistered nuns. There are touches of contemplation in every fervent Christian life. We have already noted the tension between loud praise and silent contemplation which arises in Spirit-filled charismatic prayer meetings. At times, people at prayer meetings have expressed deep regret that there are not longer periods of silence for savoring the presence of the Lord and for reflecting upon the word he has spoken.

A tension between vocal praise and silent contemplation seems to be built into the very nature of a charismatic prayer meeting, just as it is built into all good liturgy. Sincere vocal praise quickly disposes many people for quiet adoration. This is to be expected, because the *teruwah*, the festal acclamation, greets and welcomes the Lord into our midst. It focuses the people's attention directly on the Lord, in forgetfulness of self. When a person is thus lost in God and lost to self, he is open to the infusion of contemplative graces in which he experiences more fully the presence of the Lord, and falls into a deep reverence and adoration in which he is silently yielded to the Lord's work in his heart.

Of course, only the more disciplined Christians can maintain themselves very long in this silent adoration, especially when the graces of contemplation are the more subtle and delicate ones which are often mistaken for emptiness.

Moreover, at a fairly large prayer meeting, the participants are at every imaginable level of spirituality, and therefore there are always those present who are not deeply tuned to the quiet, more interior graces of God's presence. These persons become restless when there are long periods of silence, and think that nothing is happening, even though God may be working most profoundly in the hearts of many people present.

A religious sister, who prays weekly with a charismatic prayer group, wrote this in a letter to me about her experience of praise:

> At our prayer meetings there are often long periods of deep silence filled with the presence of God. Interior contemplative prayer flows from the vocal praise. Often I just want to be silent the rest of the meeting. However, at a prayer meeting one of the purposes, besides worship of God, is the building of community. The needs of everyone have to be provided for in a prayer meeting.
>
> Learning at the prayer meeting not only to praise aloud spontaneously, but also to pray interiorly, will lead people to want to spend time in such interior prayer at home, during the week.

That indeed is happening. Many of the "loud praisers" have come to me for spiritual direction concerning the interior contemplative prayer to which the Lord is drawing them.

In community prayer, there has to be something for everyone, and everyone should be patient with the needs of others for vocalization or for silence. Good community prayer has some of both, though the Holy Spirit has a way of making one or the other predominate in the whole group, depending upon the time and circumstances and his own mysterious purposes.

The prayer leader has to be delicately sensitive to his people and to the Holy Spirit, allowing silent adoration or joyous vocalization, earnest petition or grateful thanksgiving, Scripture reading or other sharing, as the Spirit leads. The ways of the Spirit are diverse, and he leads different people to praise him in different ways at different times. No one of these ways should be excluded from a Christian community, lest the whole body be impoverished.

Charismatic experience has shown that loud praise and joyous song have a power for quickly disposing hearts for a listening silence, in which the people hear the Lord speaking in the quiet of their hearts either in contemplative prayer for their own more profound personal sanctification, or in word-gifts such as prophecy and words of wisdom for the building up of the community, the Body of Christ.

Praising God aloud, then, is not the direct enemy of silent contemplation, but can be a very effective aid in disposing people for the graces of contemplation. There is a time and season for both. The silent adoration which is so often the fruit of vocal praise, and which begins in

264

the midst of the praying assembly, is to be continued and deepened in the hearts of the people as they engage in personal prayer outside the times of community prayer.

This, too, has been the perennial experience of the Church through the centuries. For example, the first followers of St. Dominic in the thirteenth century, after community prayer was ended, would prolong their worship of God in so-called "secret prayers"—the personal prayers of each of the brothers. Each would go his own way at the conclusion of the liturgical prayer of praise, continuing the fervor of prayer which had been kindled in community praise, but each expressing and deepening this fervor in whatever way was most to his liking or most profitable for him at his particular stage of spiritual growth (DS III:1529).

Contemplative Praise in the Air Force

The Spirit of God is stirring up praise in the hearts of people everywhere. Here is the witness of a young woman who is enlisted in the United States Air Force, and who has been under my spiritual guidance for several years. She writes:

> I have long been accustomed to quiet praise of God in my heart after Holy Communion, as I consider the greatness of God's Son whom I have received, and how privileged I am to receive him.
>
> Sometimes I am moved by the beauty of created things to give praise to the Creator of such splen-

dors, and to admire him for the power that enables him to keep all things in existence!

When I read the Scriptures and reflect on God's works among his people, I am moved to praise his infinite love and providence. The psalms, as songs of praise, lend themselves in a special way to my expression of this praise.

When I am alone and my surroundings are very still, I am sometimes impressed with my creature-liness, my smallness in comparison to the entire universe. I think of God and how he knows where I am; among all the objects of the universe he is able to find this small person. In an instant he fills me with grace and elevates me above all the things I imagine are so huge and great, and brings me into relationship with the Three Persons. I can sit motionless for a long time contemplating this reality, and my whole being praises God for this unique relationship. This is a wordless type of praise. It is very spontaneous, and I think it is given by God, because I cannot praise God in this way by my own decision.

This young woman in the Air Force thus witnesses to the opening statement of this chapter: the praise which is contemplation in silent adoration is not the exclusive prerogative of cloistered nuns.

CHAPTER THIRTY-THREE

The New Song Sung with the Lord's Own Voice

St. John of the Cross (died 1591) associates jubilation with the highest degree of mystical union. The second effect of the spiritual marriage or transformation in God, John says, is "Jubilation before God in the fruition of God."[53] This jubilation is the most perfect praise of God possible in this life.

St. Augustine had taught that jubilation results when one experiences God in love, and realizes that he is inexpressible. Only with God's own voice can the inexpressible be expressed. John of the Cross teaches that jubilation is the new song which God himself gives to the soul in the transforming union. The soul sings interiorly with God's own voice, which God gives to it in the highest stage of mystical union. "She sings a new and jubilant song together with God, who moves her to this. He gives his voice to her, that so united with him, she may sing to God with him."[54] "Because in this union the soul rejoices and praises God together with God himself, it is perfect praise."[55]

In the poetic imagery of *The Spiritual Canticle*, John refers to this praise as "the voice of the nightingale." The Bridegroom's own voice, resounding in the innermost substance of the Bride's soul, calls forth her voice of jubilation in response:

> She hears the sweet voice of her Beloved calling to her, and in this voice expresses to him her delightful jubilation, and calls both voices the song of the nightingale.[56]

> The bride perceives that this voice of the Spouse who speaks to her in the inmost part of her soul is the end of her ills and the beginning of her blessings. And in the refreshment and protection and delectable feeling which this causes her, she likewise lifts up her voice, like the sweet nightingale, in a new song of jubilation to God, together with God who moves her to this.[57]

> This song unites with the song that causes it. For the Bridegroom gives her a voice that she may sing to God with him, for that is his aspiration and desire.[58] This is the desire he expresses in the Song of Songs, where he says: "Arise, make haste, my love, and come my dove; in the clefts of the rock, in the hollow of the wall show me your face, let your voice sound in my ears" (Song 2:13-14). The ears of God signify his desires to have the soul sing to him with this voice of perfect jubilation. That this voice be perfect, the Bridegroom asks that she sing and let it resound in the caverns of the rock, that is, in the transformation in the mysteries of Christ.[59]

Only in Christ can we offer this perfect praise, and only when we are transformed in him.

Jubilation is the joy of being taken into the life of the Holy Trinity. For in describing jubilation, John is explaining the second of the five effects of the transforming union. In telling of the first effect, John had shown that in this union the soul breathes the same love which God breathes in his own inner life, and which he breathes forth to her and which she breathes back to him (*Spiritual Canticle* 39:3). In this love, the Bridegroom sings to her and she sings to him, and this one voice is perfect praise (39:8). The love which God breathes in himself, and to her, and which she returns to him, is the Holy Spirit:

> This breathing of the air is an ability which the soul states God will give her there in the communication of the Holy Spirit. By his divine breath-like spiration, the Holy Spirit elevates the soul sublimely and makes her capable of breathing in God the same spiration of love that the Father breathes in the Son and the Son in the Father, which is the Holy Spirit himself; who in the Father and in the Son breathes out to her in this transformation, in order to unite her to himself. There would not be a true and total transformation if the soul were not transformed in the three Persons of the Most Holy Trinity in an open and manifest degree. . . .
>
> The soul united and transformed in God breathes out in God to God the very divine spiration which God—she being transformed in him—breathes out in himself to her. . . . The same spiration passes from God to the soul and from the soul to God. . . . Such

I believe is St. Paul's meaning when he says: Since you are sons of God, God sent the Spirit of his Son into your hearts, calling to the Father (Gal.4:6).[60]

John of the Cross speaks again of jubilation in *The Living Flame of Love*:

> In this state of life so perfect (the spiritual marriage), the soul always walks in festivity, inwardly and outwardly, and it frequently bears on its spiritual tongue a new song of great jubilation in God, a song always new, enfolded in a gladness and love arising from the knowledge the soul has of its happy state ... It proclaims like the bride in the Canticle: "My Beloved belongs to me and I to Him" (Song 2:16).[61]

Praise: Christ's Own Glory in Us

John of the Cross has just told us that in the jubilation of which he speaks, the Bride praises God with the Bridegroom's own voice, for she is one with Jesus in the transforming union.

Jesus is "the glory of God." "We have beheld his glory, glory as of the only Son from the Father" (John 1:14). In him alone is perfect praise, he *is* that perfect praise, and only in him can we render that perfect praise to God. That seems to be the main thrust of what a cloistered nun was trying to say as she struggled to write for me what praise is in her life:

270

Before you began to write your book, I probably would have thought that praise has almost no place in my life. Since then I have looked a little more deeply, and have found, more or less to my own surprise, that praise is in me almost as a natural attitude; that is, I respond to it and make it my own without thinking much about it. It began to dawn on me that my heart leaps up and loves the Gloria and Sanctus at Mass, the Te Deum, the powerful expressions of praise in St. Paul, in Revelation, in the Psalms and in other places in Scripture. And so I have become more aware of the place of praise in my life.

This still doesn't say what praise is. Praise is rejoicing and thanksgiving and wonder and adoration and awe and a few other things as well, all of these in varying degrees and combinations, but not anyone of them alone, and something more than all together. We say "All the earth is filled with your glory!" or "We praise you for your great glory," and I wonder just what is this "glory"? I see it reflected all around me, I taste and experience it within me. He is filling me with his glory, transforming me from glory to glory.

St. Paul says that Jesus is the glory of the Father. And my heart can rest there, and behold his glory, the glory of the only begotten Son of the Father. I ask him to perfect his praise in my nothingness, to empty me entirely so that it may be, not I, but Jesus who lives in me, that my emptiness may reflect ever more fully the glory of God shining on the face of Christ Jesus.

All this is true and part of me; and still the

271

meaning lies even deeper. I praise him for the glorious beauty of nature, for the wonders of grace, for his tender loving care of all that is. But all of this is what St. John of the Cross calls "the groves he passed in haste." And I realize again that "all is mine and all for me, God himself is mine, because Christ is mine and all for me."

And so, at the very roots of my life, praise is for me the praise of a new bride, so much in love that the wonder of my Beloved is reflected in all that he does, and He is more wonderful than all. All my being praises him, in words or in silence, in giving or receiving, it doesn't matter much, because my love is in belonging to him totally, and the belonging is, somehow, praise. And this love never grows old. Each day brings new marvels to be explored, new depths to fathom. And each day he renews me in his love.

And suffering is not something apart from the life of praise. It does not smother it. Rather, by loving paradox, God uses it as a gateway to glory. Our Lord said, "Ought not the Christ to suffer and so enter into his glory?" I could not be open to the gift of his love, clinging to so many other things and to myself. Yet only when he begins to lead me into the fellowship of his sufferings do the depths of this mystery become more clear to me. In all the painful things, he is gradually setting me free. Somehow we penetrate the truth that he is the one who is bearing our griefs, carrying our sorrows. In this present, particular pain of mine, there is his pain, his wounding, and by it I am healed. In our very selves, the victory of life over death is being accom-

272

plished. Right now, in the midst of weakness, his glory appears!

CHAPTER THIRTY-FOUR

Love Is My Praise

"Love is my praise." These words are my summary of a cloistered nun's letter telling about praise in her life. Here are the highlights of her letter:

> *In my experience, this is what I have understood as praise, although in my conversations with God I always use the word love, not praise. I would like to say also that I think all souls, once love of God replaces fear in their lives, experience at some time a need to express audibly this praise or love of God. "From the abundance of the heart the mouth speaks."*
>
> *Just after emerging from years of a deep purification by God, at times it seemed that God would suddenly possess me with his love and my own heart would be on fire with love for him. Rarely would ever a word be spoken. My mind and soul were so absorbed in God that generally I stood motionless.... Even though I found I could not resist God when he brought his grace into my life, still I sought for some assurance that I was not*

misled. . . . One day as the priest at Mass read the words of the Gospel, "I have come not for the virtuous but for sinners," God suddenly seized my soul, and although I cannot explain it, I was united to God to an extent I have never experienced before. At the same time the words of the Gospel were my assurance, as if God said to me, "As I came for sinners, therefore I came for you, and still come to you in these impulses of love."

After this experience of God, an ever deeper peace came into my life, and in this peace I experienced a joy that God is God, a gratitude and love for God for the trials and sacrifices of my life, a greater understanding of these trials and sacrifices, and a greater understanding, love and gratitude for God giving me the gift of life and sacraments. I began to long for the opportunity to speak of this gratitude, love and understanding to God, and I think this is where audible praise came into my conversation with God. It seemed I could not contain within my heart and soul this need, and so I sought out some remote place among the surroundings of nature to speak my love of God. I used to go out a distance from the house and, standing among the tall trees, would speak aloud my love and gratitude to God. Many graces of love and deep peace came to me.

After some time I began to understand how far removed this was from speaking face to face with God, although I knew he heard me. Indeed, I could never have said the words if He had not allowed me. And so my desires to be with God became more and more intense.

One day it seemed to me that God said to me, or made me to understand, that I could speak to him in the sacraments. And so a greater longing for the sacraments came into my life. I spoke to the confessor who knew me well, and he gave me leave to speak from my heart to God whenever our Lord gave me that attraction. I think the new rite for confession greatly facilitates this.

With this audible speaking to God there has come a lightness or freedom of soul, along with three special graces: a love for the sacraments; a love of Scripture—at times it seems our Lord is speaking to me (a few times as the Scriptures were being read at Mass, it seemed as if, or rather intellectually I could see, a hand writing the words in my heart). Finally, recently, a sense of anticipation of the joy, rather than embarrassment, of standing before God and the elect in eternity (I suppose at the last judgment), and all seeing the goodness of God to me and how little I deserved it. This means they will know my sins and infidelities, and there is joy in their knowing them, because in this knowing, God's mercy will also be better known and loved. These desires have made me understand that part of St. Therese of the Child Jesus' oblation: "until the shadows fall and I can tell him my love face to face."

In response to my sister's letter I hasten to pray: "May the Lord grant you your heart's desire, and refuse you not the wish of your lips" (Ps.21:3). The desires written in your heart by his own word and Spirit are the ones he will fulfill, if you offer your heart in the continuing praise which is love.

For he hears not just shouts of praise. He hears the deepest desires of our hearts, the ones implanted at the very roots of our being by the Spirit, who helps our weakness by interceding for us with sighs too deep for words, inspiring in our hearts the desires which God wills to fulfill, desires for things which we would never have dreamed of asking or have dared to ask if he himself had not inspired the desire for them (Rom.8:26-27). With those who love God—in the marvelous praise which is loving surrender to His love—he works in everything for their good (Rom.8:28).

This love and desire is magnificent praise, because it is the only adequate response and witness to his love. In this desire, all our other desires are borne before him, purified and caught up into and integrated into the one great desire: "to tell him my love face to face." "Take delight in the Lord, and he will give you your heart's desire" (Ps.37:4).

NOTES

1. *Sermons* 34:1,6 (PL 38:210-211).
2. *On Psalm 147*, 3 (PL 37:1916).
3. *Sermons* 34:6 (PL 38:211).
4. *L'Osservatore Romano* (English edition), Oct. 7, 1972.
5. *Dictionnaire de Spiritualite*, Tome VIII (Paris: Beauchesne, 1975), Col. 1471-77.
6. *Confessions of St. Augustine*, translated by F. J. Sheed (New York: Sheed and Ward, 1943), pp.212-213.
7. *The Interior Castle*, St. Teresa of Avila, translated by E. Allison Peers (New York: Sheed and Ward, 1946), pp.301-302. Doubleday Image edition, pp. 167-169.
8. Bede, *Homilies* 1:4.
9. Paul VI, *Marialis Cultis*, para.11, Feb.2, 1974.
10. In quotations from St. Augustine's commentaries on the psalms, we have in most cases made our own translation. But even when we have done this, we give a reference to one or the other of two commonly available translations. When we have used these translations, we have done so with the permission of the copyright owners. In the references in this chapter and the next, we shall refer to these translations as A and B:

A. *Ancient Christian Writers*, vol. 29 and 30: *St. Augustine on the Psalms*, translated and annotated by Hebgin and Corrigan (Westminster: Newman, 1961).

B. *The Nicene and Post-Nicene Fathers*, vol 8: *St. Augustine, Expositions on the Book of Psalms* (Grand Rapids: Eerdmans, 1956).

Our reference for the present quotation is to B,pp.468,488, n.4.
11. A, vol. 30, p.111.
12. A, vol.30, p.111
13. B, p.488,n.4
14. B, p.433, n.16
15. A, vol.30, pp.272-273

16. B, p.488, n.5-6

17. *The Confessions of St. Augustine*, Sheed, p.150.

18. B, p.274, n.2.

19. A, vol.30, p.273.

20. A, vol.29, p.258.

21. Eddie Ensley, "Healing and Worship in the Fifth Century Church," *New Covenant*, March 1975, pp.15-17.

22. Ibid.

23. Ibid.

24. Ibid.

25. *The Confessions of St. Augustine*, Sheed, p.210.

26. PL 76:292a.

27. B, p.490, n.10.

28. Roland de Vaux, *Ancient Israel: Its Life and Institutions* (New York: McGraw-Hill, 1961), p.417.

29. Ibid.

30. Thomas Worden, *The Psalms Are Christian Prayer* (New York: (Sheed and Ward, 1961), pp.60-72.

31. *The Confessions of St. Augustine*, Sheed, p.210.

32. Ibid., p.3.

33. Ibid., p.212.

34. Ibid., p.213.

35. Ibid.

36. Ibid.

37. Ibid., p.214.

38. Ibid., p.257.

39. Ibid., p.211.

40. A, vol.30, p.160.

41. Prayer before the priest's communion.

42. A, vol.30, p.272.

43. *The Confessions of St. Augustine*, Sheed, p.352.

44. M. M. Philipon, *The Spiritual Doctrine of Sister Elizabeth of the Trinity*, (Westminster: Newman, 1955), p.232.

45. Regina Mundi Priory, Devon, Pennsylvania.

46. *The Confessions of St. Augustine*, Sheed, p.214.

47. Ibid., p.256.

48. Ibid., p.257.

49. Selected sentences from Elizabeth's last retreat notes, slightly paraphrased and rearranged for harmonious reading. Philipon, *The Spiritual Doctrine of Sister Elizabeth of the Trinity*, p.234.

50. Madeleine Delbrel, *We the People of the Streets* (Paris: Ed. du Seuil, 1966), pp.89-92. This translation from *Christian Readings*, vol. 4 (New York: Catholic Book Publishing Co., 1973). Used with permission.

51. John of the Cross, *The Spiritual Canticle* 20:2

52. Ibid., 38:8-9.

53. In quotations from St. John of the Cross, we have drawn on two translations. In the references, we shall refer to these translations as C and D:

C. *The Complete Works of St. John of the Cross*, vol. 2, translated and edited by E. Allison Peers (Westminster: Newman, 1953).

D. *The Collected Works of St. John of the Cross*, translated by Kieran Kavanaugh and Otilio Rodriguez (Washington: Institute of Carmelite Studies, 1964).

Our reference for the present quotation is to c, p. 374.

54. D, p.560.

55. C, p.171.

56. D, pp.559-560.

57. C, pp.377-378.

58. Ibid., p.170.

59. D, p.560.

60. Ibid., p.558.

61. Ibid., p.609.